KNITTING FROM THE
NETHERLANDS

Henriette van der Klift-Tellegen

KNITTING FROM THE NETHERLANDS

TRADITIONAL DUTCH FISHERMEN'S SWEATERS

Lark Books
Asheville, North Carolina

Drawings: Hetty Paerl
Layout and design: Karel van Laar
Photographs of knitted swatches:
Henriette C. van der Klift-Tellegen
Translated from the Dutch by Marianne Wiegman

Opposite title page: Two fishermen from
Scheveningen and two from Urk (seated), wearing the
sweaters typical of their villages.

Back cover: Two children from Volendam

Published in 1985 by Lark Books,
a division of Lark Communications Corporation
50 College Street
Asheville, North Carolina 28801

First published in the Netherlands under the title
Nederlandse visserstruien
© Uitgeverij Cantecleer bv, de Bilt 1983
English translation © 1985
by Lark Books

Library of Congress Catalog Card Number:
85 – 50780

ISBN 0-937274-17-8

Printed in the Netherlands

Contents

Introduction

During the past ten years there has been a growing interest in traditional sweaters from other countries. Many of them, now worn for skiing, sailing, or bicycling, were originally fishermen's sweaters. The wearers are convinced that such sweaters are superior when it comes to warmth and freedom of movement. The Irish and Fair Isle fishermen's sweaters, and the Norwegian sweaters, have even entered the ateliers of the fashion designers. How and why this trend developed is unknown, but it is apparent that the knitters in those countries are profiting from it. The most beautiful and most original sweaters are not created in the knitting mills, but on the needles of local knitters. And nothing is superior to the quality of the original handwork.

This interest in ethnic knitting inspired me to begin a search in the Netherlands. After all, our country is well known for its fishing industry, and was also once famous for its knitting. So what about traditional Dutch fishermen's sweaters? The first reaction of people with whom I discussed this idea was astonishment: "Dutch fishermen's sweaters? I've never heard of such a thing!" Nor were people in the fishing villages convinced that there was anything unique about their sweaters: "*Special* fishermen's sweaters? No, we do not have anything like that. We just have plain ones that used to be knitted here in the village." All those negative reactions annoyed me. Why shouldn't those sweaters be special? Why does something have to be imported in order to be considered special?

The idea was born and the research could now begin. For three years I roamed through the Netherlands, from Moddergat to Vlissingen, and spoke with dozens of people. On their faces I first read puzzlement at my questions, but then came an awakening interest. Archivists researched their collections, others their boxes of photographs. What appeared surprised everybody. I received picture after picture of fishermen wearing beautiful sweaters. Many fishing villages appeared to have had their own particular sweater designs. At times the pictures came from unexpected sources. In the archives of Middelburg the photographs I wanted were not found in the drawer labelled "costumes" but in the one marked "shipwrecks." Elsewhere they were filed under "harbor views." After while it became apparent that the pessimists were wrong. There *were* beautiful sweaters that had been worn by Dutch fishermen. But they were worn for a relatively short period of time and now are nearly extinct. In only a few places were they still being worn. If these designs are to be preserved, speed is of the essence.

Further research showed that nowhere were the patterns written down; the women stated that they were simply taught by their mothers. The motif and the pattern were copied from an existing sweater. The new one was an exact replica, or had some slight variation. It is difficult for us, living in the time of the printed word, to comprehend this. Everything we make requires a written pattern and a diagram.

People used to remember all acquired knowledge. Their memories were better trained than ours are now, and knowledge was passed orally from one person to another. They were convinced that, should they forget a bit of information, it would be really forgotten and lost to the generations after them. Because of the change in times this nearly did happen to the knitting patterns. The advantage to this oral tradition was that people were freer. No designer or expert gave instructions. A variation on an existing pattern was made without any fuss or concern for whether it was "allowed." The much-proclaimed creativity, about which we now speak so often and in which courses are taught, was at that time referred to simply as "thinking of something." Because of that thinking of something, original knitted pieces were created, pieces which we now admire greatly. Of course they were not created in a day; the process developed very slowly. Someone thought to cross stitches, and in time many cable variations evolved.

This book contains a collection of original fishermen's sweaters with a truly unique character. The patterns were created in a time when the people had very little communication outside their own villages. The patterns are therefore quite local. A knitter who makes one of these sweaters can, of course, adhere

C. van Wijk: Little girl knitting. Collection of the City Museum of The Hague.

strictly to the local patterns and motifs, but it would be a shame for the early designs to become law.

Small, personal variations give the knitted piece an individual touch without changing the overall appearance. Also the knitting in of initials, or the use of some small inconspicuous motifs, can add a special look.

In a number of villages which had fishing fleets I was unable to find evidence of local sweater patterns even though I suspect they existed. If those of you with Dutch ancestors have in your possession photographs in which old fishermen's sweaters are clearly identifiable, please contact me. I hope this book will inspire new interest in the Dutch knitting heritage and that many of you will knit, and wear with pride, a Dutch fisherman's sweater.

Henriette C. van der Klift-Tellegen

7

Origin and History

The History of Knitting

The art of knitting is very old, so old that it is difficult to trace its beginnings. It is possible that weaving and knitting originated at about the same time.

In early times especially, the two techniques complemented each other. Straight pieces were woven; circular ones knitted. Knitwear was stretchable; woven material was not. We have a hard time imagining this today, because from straight pieces we now are able to sew round ones, and we can knit flat. But even today the two techniques are used together for the same reason.

There are many legends and stories about knitting and its origin. One legend tells of Eve in Paradise, knitting socks for Adam and using the pattern of the snake's back in her work.

In Yemen it is believed that knitting always existed, even before the time of the Queen of Sheba. In other tales she is named as the inventor of knitting. In any case it is certain that the technique of knitting is very old. Knitted pieces dating back to 1100 A.D. have been found in Egypt.

The Arabs were the first to develop knitting techniques. They knitted in a fashion similar to the way fishing nets are made. The only difference from today's technique for knitting nets is that the Arabs

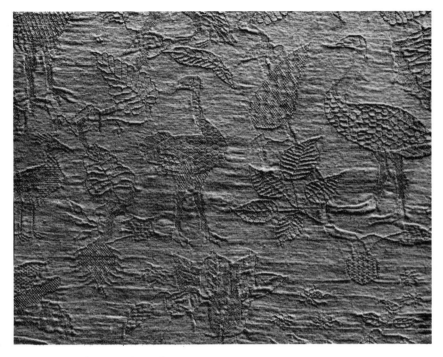

▲ Early Dutch knitting. From the collection of the Victoria and Albert Museum, London.

did not fasten the loops with a knot, but tightened the thread in such a way that a compact structure was created. They knitted sandal socks, footwear well suited to walking in the hot, loose sand of the desert. Examples of such socks, from about 100 A.D., are on exhibit in several museums.

Originally knitting and weaving were trades for men. As far back as the Middle Ages there were knitters' guilds, with strict requirements for membership. A young man had to be an apprentice for about six years,

then to finish his apprenticeship with the creation of a masterpiece.

The English apprentices at that time wore knitted caps resembling those of the Egyptian Christians, the Copts. It is believed that when they brought Christianity to Europe they also brought the craft of knitting. Dutch knitters had a special knitting style, different from that of surrounding countries.

The Dutch knitted decorative patterns in low relief, without using a second color or crossed stitches. During the 15th and 16th centuries the Netherlands set the pace in the craft of knitting. By 1429 knitting guilds had been formed and were producing high-quality knitwear.

Tsar Peter I (1672-1725) travelled with his family and servants to Doornik, a town famous for its knitting, to order clothing and distinctive high-crowned knitted hats. He presented one of those hats as a royal gift to the Pope, which indicates how precious knitwear was at that time.

Another popular story is that, around 1550, the king of Denmark was so impressed with the superior quality and fit of the Dutch stock-ings that he brought a group of Dutch knitters and their families to Denmark to introduce the art of stocking knitting. The king issued a law, proclaiming that only he and his royal household were allowed to wear silk stockings. The burghers of Copenhagen rebelled, and the king then allowed them to wear cotton stockings. Then the common people rebelled, so the king ordered them to wear woolen stockings. By looking at a person's legs one could determine the class to which he belonged.

A stocking knitter with some skill earned a decent income. So to increase their profits, Dutch mer-chants had their stockings knitted in northern England and Scotland at a lower cost. Perhaps it was to stop this exploitation that a poor minister, William Lee, invented the knitting machine in about 1598.

There are many theories as to the reason the knitting machine was invented. It was said that Lee fell in love with a woman who knitted

▲ Hat belonging to Peter I, made in the Netherlands. Hermitage Museum, Leningrad.

woolen stockings. Because she showed more interest in her knitting than in his advances, he constructed a machine that made it unnecessary for her to spend so much time at her knitting. By then, knitting was already a women's occupation. The skilled, well paid knitters made lacy silk stockings, while the women working for minimum wage made woolen stockings for the common people.

There is another story about Lee meeting his sweetheart at a secret place, where they could finally be alone. The girl, however, had brought her knitting along, and he was unable to keep her attention. He became very angry, and he swore to invent a machine that would eliminate her source of income.

Although the reason for William Lee's invention is not totally clear, the date is more certain. In the 1590s he developed the first knit-ting machine and thereby changed the course of knitting history. From the first it appeared that this ma-chine would fulfill a need: to free the underpaid women from the tedium of stocking knitting. But Queen Elizabeth I would not grant Lee a patent for his invention and prohibited further development of the machine. Lee and his family moved to France. He did not have much success there, either, and died in 1610 a disappointed man.

Lee's brother continued work on the machine, and improved the original model. He installed the first knitting machine in Leiden, in the Netherlands, and frame knitting of stockings began. Queen Elizabeth's prediction came true: the stocking knitters were outdone by the machine and the trade disappeared.

After that, knitting became a household craft and was no longer a trade for men. Only the fishermen and herdsmen continued to knit. In some cases they knitted to make money; in others they knitted just for pleasure. Women continued to knit professionally. Older women still do earn extra money this way, but no one today can earn a living from it.

Origin of the Fishermen's Sweaters

Originally, Dutch fishermen's sweaters were probably worn as undervests, beautifully made garments that might have been worn over an undershirt and under a smock or jacket. It used to be common to work in just one's "underwear," so the sweater often was visible. We can assume, then, that the fisherman's sweater evolved from under- to outerwear, as has happened more recently with the T-shirt.

There is a strong resemblance between the Dutch fishermen's sweaters and those worn in the British Isles. As long ago as the 14th century the Dutch had contact with the Shetland Islands, England and Scotland. In 1312 a procedure was discovered for curing herring. Fishermen could then preserve their catch for longer periods of time and became free to search for richer fishing grounds located farther away from the coast.

Around 1500 the Dutch whalers began to trade food for Shetland Island sweaters, which they wore as underwear. The ancestors of the Shetland Islanders came from Norway and they knitted their sweaters of wool in natural colors. In the archives on the Shetland Islands are knitted fragments that

support this theory, but complete sweaters from that period have never been found.

During the fishing season the Dutch fishermen used to make their base on the Shetland Islands, where the people were kinder to them than were the English or the Scots. The fact that the Dutch used their fishing grounds was often the cause of hostility and fighting.

Because of the close contact between the two nationalities, each influenced the other's clothing. The Shetland Islanders wore their sweaters as outerwear, but it wasn't until the time of the French occupation that the Dutch fishermen adopted this custom.

During the French occupation in the beginning of the 19th century the fishing industry in the Netherlands was nearly nonexistent. Contact with the British Isles was interrupted by the economic boycott of the French under Napoleon. Then around 1860 the fishing industry blossomed once again. The lugger made its appearance, as did the tight-meshed cotton fishing nets. The political situation was more stable. Consequently, commerce was renewed with the English, Scots and Shetland Islanders, and at that time the Dutch fishermen began to wear sweaters as outerwear.

The motifs knitted into the sweaters were related to the sea and the fishing industry (see "Motifs" on page 19). The knitters passed along their patterns from generation to generation. Often the motifs were

▲ Young girl from the village of Urk knitting in front of her house.

to those knitted by hand. Machine-made sweaters were distinguishable by their even knitting and singular motif in the center front. These sweaters were made in England and Belgium especially for the Dutch fishermen. North Sea fishermen wore English-made sweaters with the God's Eye motif; regular service bargemen wore Belgian sweaters with an anchor design. It is likely that these sweaters were worn earlier than the hand-knitted ones, because knitting by machine had been common practice since about 1650.

The origin of the British fishermen's sweater is somewhat clearer than is that of the Dutch. They were designed to replace the smocks, workmen's shirts similar to the smocks in other European countries. All craftsmen wore, until the start of this century, handwoven linen smocks. To give the wearer sufficient freedom of movement the smocks were gathered in the front and back. The gathers were sewn in place with embroidery stitches that were elastic as well as decorative.

This technique of elastic embroidery is called smocking, after the garment. Traditionally, the symbols embroidered on the garment indicated the wearer's occupation. Many English museums have beautiful smocks in their collections. The Victoria and Albert Museum in London contains magnificent examples, of which some of the finest are the wedding smocks. During her engagement the bride-

knitted only in the top half of the sweater. This was done, in difficult times, to save yarn. Plain knitting requires considerably less yarn than does knitting with a motif. Cables, especially, are very "uneconomical" motifs.

The children of fishermen first learned to knit by making stockings and hats in stockinette stitch: one row of knitting then one of purling. Then they learned to knit motifs. Only after they became proficient in knitting motifs were they allowed to knit sweaters. Fishermen wore machine-knit sweaters in addition to-be embroidered an especially elaborate smock for her groom. He wore it only on the wedding day, then it was carefully packed away.

The British fishermen also wore smocks, originally under jackets of sea-lion fur. Later, heavy knitted sweaters replaced the smocks. Those first sweaters were knitted to resemble smocks as closely as possible. On the front and back yoke of the sweater were knitted patterns with a gathering effect, such as cables. On both sides of the cables were sections with symbolic stitches. The tradition of the wedding smock lived on. The bride-elect of a fisherman began, as soon as she was engaged, to knit a special sweater for her groom. The sweater was worn on the wedding day, and afterward on Sundays and holidays.

This tradition was also common in the Netherlands. In Scheveningen, near The Hague, a bride began to knit on the day her wedding date was set.

▲ Fisherman from Scheveningen, wearing an original smock.

Identification

In the time when passports and drivers' licenses were unknown, a simple means of identification was of the utmost importance. When in foreign ports, it was necessary for a person's nationality to be apparent. People were not often fluent in each other's languages, and communication was difficult. In the event of an accident or other mishap identification was necessary. The most common way to identify a person was by his clothing and footwear. Because clothing had specific distinguishing characteristics, people were recognized by strangers as well as by their own countrymen. With fishermen, sweaters played an important role as identification. The colors were significant, so were the application and combination of motifs. The Dutch fishermen wore sweaters with motifs that were unique to their localities. In many cases it was possible to identify a drowned fisherman by the motifs of his sweater, even after a long stay in the water. His body could then be shipped back to his home port or his family could be notified.

This method of identification was used in most European harbors. Motifs knitted on the sweaters related to either the fisherman's home port or his family. Sometimes, as in Bretagne, it was not the motifs that identified the wearer's home, but the colors. The color combinations and width of the stripes on sweaters differed from port to port. In Ireland the motifs differed from one family to the next. In the Irish sweaters knitted motifs also carried messages. A motif might indicate the number of sons in the family, or convey the seriousness of the knitter's religious beliefs.

On the isle of Jersey the emblems of the different parishes were knitted into the fronts of the sweaters, while the rest was knitted plain.

The Guernsey sweaters were plain except for a few details. On the shoulders were bands of garter stitch, and at the bottom there was a border of garter stitch instead of the usual ribbed border.

The Scottish and English sweaters had a combination of motifs that differed from port to port. The traditional Norwegian sweaters are exceptional in that they were designed not by fishermen, but by herdsmen. The motifs used on them varied according to the valley where they were made. Identification was a factor here, too.

These are only a few examples of the sweaters made throughout time for fishermen. Their role as identification is no longer so important, because, since the beginning of the 19th century, fishing boats have carried a registration number which identifies the home port. At that time it also became popular to knit monograms into sweaters.

Even today, in strange harbors, fishermen recognize each other by their sweaters. Sweaters worn by the Dutch fishermen are distinguishable by the combination of knitted motifs. Each fishing village had its own motifs. The sweaters were nearly always black or dark blue, in a few cases marine blue or even gray. The combination of motifs was standard from location to location. Even so, research shows that knitters used some imagination. The panels between the motifs differed, or the number of motifs varied. Some knitted their initials, or those of their husbands, in the sweaters. In these and many other small ways they incorporated individuality into the sweaters, which, if seen from a distance, all looked alike.

Materials and Techniques

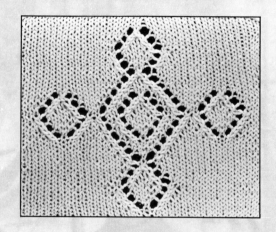

Sajet

For the original fishermen's sweaters an all-wool yarn called *sajet* (pronounced sah-YET) was used. Sajet was very popular among the fishing population, but was a household word in the rest of the country as well. Stockings, underwear and sweaters were knitted from it, because in addition to being inexpensive it was readily available. In every country store one could buy sajet; in places without stores it was offered by the traveling peddlers. Opinions as to the quality and durability of sajet differed. With wear, sajet acquired a sheen, which was not to everyone's liking. To really appreciate sajet it is necessary to look back to the times when all available material had to be used.

Farmers' wives brought the fleece of their sheep to the spinning mills to sell for yarn making. But not all sheep produce wool that is good for yarn. Through the centuries advances in breeding techniques have produced sheep raised specifically for meat, or milk, or wool. The wool of a sheep bred for that purpose, like the Merino, is long and soft. Yarn spun from it is strong, and also stays soft, because it need not be tightly spun.

The wool of a sheep bred for meat, such as the Dutch Texelaar, from the island of Texel, is short and fairly rough. To spin good yarn from it, it must be tightly twisted. The technical term, in Dutch, for this firm twist is *sajet*. Because this wool was grown domestically and was available in large quantities, the price was low. As long as people had to be thrifty, sajet was popular. After World War II the standard of living improved and people were able to afford more expensive yarns. The sajet disappeared.

The introduction of cheaper synthetic yarns played a role in sajet's fall from popularity. When sajet disappeared, so did the typical sajet colors, Nassau blue and Nassau beige. Nassau is the name of the Dutch royal family. In addition to those colors, sajet also was dyed black, dark blue and gray. The Nassau blue was a blue yarn into which small red threads were spun, giving the blue yarn a reddish hue. Not everyone cared for this color, and in certain parts of the country, Nassau blue was a color worn only by poor people. In other places Nassau blue was used only for stockings; for sweaters one knitted with the "good" sajet in black or blue.

On the islands of Zuidholland Nassau blue was an esteemed color, and was preferred for sweater knitting. After the war, when sajet disappeared, fishermen's wives knitted the sweaters from stocking wool. Today synthetic yarns also are used for fishermen's sweaters.

Motifs

Many fishermen's sweaters began their long lives as part of the costume of men whose own lives were full of danger and hardship. There were many unforeseen events at sea. A fisherman depended on the weather, yet he could not forecast it with any certainty. A seasoned fisherman understood cloud formations and winds, but it was impossible for him to really know what to expect. Fog might appear suddenly; a storm might change the wind direction and catch a fishing boat by surprise A long calm period might make it impossible for sailboats to navigate. For no particular reason the fish might refuse to swim into the nets. It was not without reason that fishermen threw out their nets with the traditional words "Good hope!"

Their dependence on the elements made fishermen highly superstitious. The motifs worked into their clothes had deep symbolic meaning. The oldest are the motifs from Ireland, some of which were adopted and worn by the Dutch seafarers.

Flower or God's Eye

This motif is centuries old and appears in a number of different cultures. It is impossible to trace its origin, but is known to have been used by the Celts and by the Incas.

It is also found in the artwork of the Copts. In many different languages it has the same name: Eye of God, *Ojo de Dios* and *Godsoog,* to name a few. That eye symbolizes the eye which sees everything our eyes cannot, and observes everything that we cannot perceive.

The God's Eye motif is used on the Dutch sweaters. In Urk, which was an island in the Zuider Zee, this same motif is called a *flower,* even though the earlier meaning is not completely forgotten. This motif is said to bring good luck. At times it is also called a *diamond,* and symbolizes prosperity. It is interesting that the machine-made fishermen's sweaters carry only this motif; all others are omitted.

In some areas of the country, the name God's Eye is well known, but the meaning is somewhat different. A woman in IJmuiden, one of the fishing villages, told us: "That eye looks after the men in strange ports

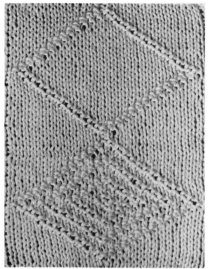

▲ God's Eye from Pernis or Urk.

so they will conduct themselves properly. It used to be common, in a bar, to find a wall plaque with an eye painted on it. Under it were the words 'God sees you,' meant as a warning to the patrons." The eye then was a warning symbol instead of a protective one. Another woman explained: "Men often cannot tell front from back. The design is in the front and the back is smooth, therefore even in the dark a man can put such a sweater on with the right side to the front."

This motif, on Dutch sweaters, is made with purl stitches. The God's Eye used on English sweaters is a combination of knit stitches and small eyelets. An eyelet is made by wrapping the yarn around the needle and then knitting two stitches together, or by knitting two stitches together then wrapping the yarn.

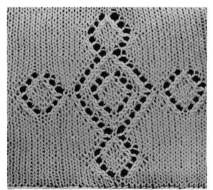

▲ God's Eye, English sweater

Cable

Cables appeared often in the sweaters of fishermen. The symbolism is obvious: no ship could sail without cables and ropes. They are motifs which depict the essentials of navigation. How to knit cables:

Cable to the right: knitted over 6 stitches
Row 1: P1, K4, P1.
Row 2: K1, P4, K1.
Row 3: P1, sl 2 sts onto cable needle and leave at front of work, K2, K2 sts from cable needle, P1.
Row 4: K1, P4, K1.

Cable to the left: knitted over 6 stitches
Row 1: P1, K4, P1.
Row 2: K1, P4, K1.

Row 3: P1, sl 2 sts onto cable needle and leave at back of work, K2, K2 sts from cable needle, P1
Row 4: K1, P4, K1.

Flags

The flag motif appears often, and is also common on sweaters from Scotland. This motif consists of knit and purl stitches. In Urk, however, flags were called *points*. Before the discovery of radio, fishermen used flags to communicate. The colors and location of the flags told a necessary tale. For example, a boat could report the size of its catch. Or that a crew member was ill, or had died. The ability to send and receive flag signals was, in earlier days, of the utmost importance. Today, in the Netherlands, Flag Day is a special holiday on which all the fishing boats are decked out with their flags.

Tree of Life

The Tree of Life, with its many branches, symbolizes the generations. The father is the trunk and the branches are the sons. This motif appears often on Irish sweaters. The daughters were omitted, not because they were unimportant, but because they belonged to their mothers. A mother taught her daughters her skills, while a father taught his sons. In the Netherlands fishermen began the education and training of their small sons at an early age; from the seventh year the boys accompanied their fathers to sea. This motif is used both horizontally and vertically and it consists of knit and purl stitches.

Right   Left

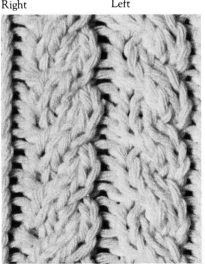

▼ Flags

▼ Tree of Life

▲ Arrows or V-forms

Arrows or V-Forms

These motifs also are made with knit and purl stitches. They depict the wakes of fast-moving ships. Harpoon points also were this shape. These and the other images were never seen by the fishermen's homebound wives. Therefore it is likely that the men themselves created the first authentic fishermen's knitwear, and through it, depicted their world.

Garter Stitch Bands

The bands of garter stitch represent sand ridges on the beach. At low tide sharp ridges appear in the sand. This motif consists of knit and purl stitches. Bands of garter

▼ Garter stitch

stitch were commonly used on the sweaters from the village of Katwijk.

Waves

Also composed of knit and purl stitches, this motif symbolizes the waves of the sea. It appears in many variations. Waves are found in particular on the sweaters from Vlaardingen and the surrounding areas.

▲ Waves

Fishbone

The motif is made up of knit and purl stitches. Its connection with the fishing industry is clear.

▲ Fishbone

The Zigzag or Lightning Bolt

Many meanings are attached to this knit/purl motif. Sometimes it is called a *snake* and serves as a warning to prowling evil. It is also known as the Lightning Bolt. Anyone who has ever been at sea during heavy storms can attest to the ferocity of lightning. The Marriage Line is another name, signifying the ups and downs of marriage.

▲ Zigzag or Lightning Bolt

21

Continuous Diamonds

This motif also has different meanings. In some places it is called

▼ Continuous diamonds

the Fishnet. In the village of Arnemuiden this motif is also found in the walls of buildings. In a time when it was impossible to bake a large quantity of bricks of the same color, bricklayers made diamond patterns in the walls to show off the different colors. Knit and purl stitches are used.

Braidstitch
Multiple of 8 stitches.
Row 1: P1, K6, P1.
Row 2: K1, P6, K1.
Row 3: P1, K2, sl 2 sts onto cable needle and hold in front of work, K2, K2 from cable needle, P1.
Row 4: K1, P6, K1.
Row 5: P1, K6, P1.
Row 6: K1, P6, K1.
Row 7: P1, sl 2 sts onto cable needle and hold in back of work, K2, K2 from cable needle, K2, P1.
Row 8: K1, P6, K1.

Bobbles or Blackberry Stitch
Row 1: P1, K 3 sts in the next st as follows: K1, P1, K1 without dropping the loop, P next 3 sts together as 1 st, repeat to end of needle.
Row 2: P.
Row 3: As row 1 but staggered; 3 sts out of one above the stitch knitted together, and 3 sts together over the increase stitch.
Row 4: same as row 2.

▼ Braidstitch

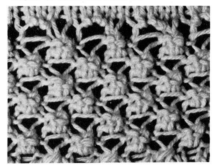

▲ Bobbles or Blackberry Stitch

Small Blocks
This motif was knitted differently in various places. On the island of Texel it is P4, K4 staggered; in Arnemuiden it is a small stockinette square bordered by purl stitches. The design had no particular significance in the Netherlands, but in Ireland it was called Jacob's Ladder after the Bible story about Jacob's climb to heaven.

▲ Small Blocks

The fishermen's sweaters from other countries, especially those from the Aran Islands, had many motifs which were not adopted by the Dutch. Examples include the Trinity Stitch, the Crab Claw, the Blarney Kiss, and the cross. The reason might be that these symbols were of a strictly local nature, or that they were symbols for the religion of the fishermen in that place. Of the motifs, the meanings of the symbols that were adopted by the Dutch were often unknown, perhaps because the fishermen did not speak or understand each others' languages very well. Communication was usually limited to a few easy sentences; conversations involving intangibles were nearly impossible.

Techniques

The original method of knitting a sweater was with four or more needles. In the Netherlands this method is still used today. The fishermen's wives, especially, have maintained the tradition. They believe that an authentic fisherman's sweater is knitted in such a way that needle and thread are never used. It is surprising to note, however, that sweaters other than the traditional fishermen's sweaters were knitted in the more conventional manner: in separate pieces which were then stitched together.

The same size needles were used for the entire sweater, including the ribbing. The result was that the ribbing rolled up when the sweater was worn.

Women never wrote down any of the knitting outlines, patterns or stitches. The patterns and the instructions in this book were all taken directly from the old photographs, thus have the problems and limitations of the original sweaters.

The pattern measurements were calculated by using a simple but effective technique. All measurements and stitch counts were divided by three. The division of the shoulders and the neck, for example, was done as follows: one third of the total number of stitches was one shoulder, one third the neck, and one third the second shoulder. The armhole began at one third of the total length of the bodice. This method of calculation is simple to apply and easy to remember.

To determine the number of stitches to be cast on, the chest measurement was used with about 2¼ inches added for ease. Then a gauge swatch about 4 inches square was knitted, and the number of stitches per inch multiplied by the number of inches needed for the width of the sweater.

This system is still used today, and is followed as closely as possible in this book, except for width. The traditional fishermen's sweaters were molded to the body. That is no longer the fashion, so an ease of about 3 to 5 inches has been added to the width in these patterns. *Always knit a gauge swatch to calculate the correct number of stitches.*

All of the fishermen's sweaters are the same style; the only variation is in the motifs and their arrangement. Calculation and adaptation of the motifs to these patterns will not be difficult for a somewhat seasoned knitter. On the drawings, large sections of stockinette stitch are left white. To fit the motifs into the number of stitches which you have calculated for your own sweater, it is best to eliminate the motif bands on both sides under the armhole, or to make them narrower or wider. The sweater drawings marked with a dark dot are difficult to re-size unless you are a skilled knitter, and those patterns are all calculated at a men's medium size.

Materials

The traditional sweaters were of wool, and were knitted very tightly. Use sport weight or light worsted weight yarn, such as Neveda Toledo or Scheepjeswol Superwash Zermatt.

Use the needle size with which you obtain the correct gauge. The following are approximate:
Circular needles numbers 2 and 3 or 4
4 double-pointed needles, numbers 2 and 3 or 4.
2 straight needles, number 3 or 4.

Gauge

Make a gauge swatch 4 x 4 inches. Gauge: in stockinette, 6 sts = 1 inch; 8 rows = 1 inch.

Stitches

Stockinette Stitch
Flat knitting: Row 1: K
Row 2: P.
Circular knitting: all rows K.

Garter Stitch
Flat knitting: all rows K
Circular knitting: 1st row K, 2nd row P

Ribbing
Row 1: K1, P1
Row 2: K above the K in previous row, P above P or:
Row 1: K2, P2.
Row 2: K above K, P above P

Seed Stitch
Row 1: K1, P1
Row 2: P above K in previous row, K above P
See the preceding pages for instructions for the different motifs.

Patent Stitch
Multiple of 2 stitches

Row 1: *K1, yarn over, slip 1 stitch. Repeat from * and finish the row with K2.
Row 2 and all succeeding rows: K1, * yarn over, slip 1, K the next stitch together with the yarn over from the previous row. Repeat from * and end with K1.

Instructions
With number 2 needles, cast on the number of stitches calculated with your gauge swatch. Knit 2″ in ribbing pattern (K1, P1). Change to number 3 or 4 needles and choose the motifs. Follow the chosen pattern up to the armhole (see the specific pattern graph). Divide the piece in two parts and knit each one separately to the desired length. Note: the drawings are based on the use of a circular needle, and show only the right side of the pattern. If straight needles are used, be sure, when reading the graph, to make the necessary adjustments for wrong side rows.

Front
Divide the number of stitches in three and put the stitches for the neck on a stitch holder or length of yarn. Knit to the shoulders, and put those stitches on stitch holders.

Back
Knit to the neckline, and divide the stitches in three. Knit the stitches for the back shoulder together with the stitches of the front shoulder as follows: pick up 1 stitch from the front and 1 from the back and K these together. Do this with the next two stitches, then pass the previous stitch over. In this manner, bind off the shoulder. Bind off the other shoulder the same way.

Neck
Pick up the stitches from the stitch holder and from around the neckline. Knit a ribbing about 1½″. Bind off.

Sleeves
Pick up stitches around the armhole, and knit the design you have chosen. Make decreases in the undersleeve according to the pattern. When the sleeve is the desired length, change to number 2 needles and knit ribbing for about 2″. Bind off.

Symbols

| | knit
− | purl
cable to right
cable to left
∧ | 2 stitches together
⋏ | slip 1 stitch, knit 1, and pass the slipped stitch over
⋀ | slip 1, knit 2 stitches together, pass the slipped stitch over
⋀ | 3 stitches together
· | yarn over

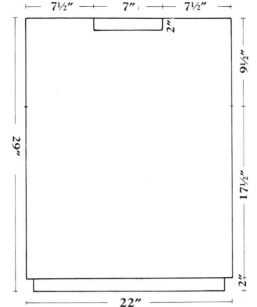

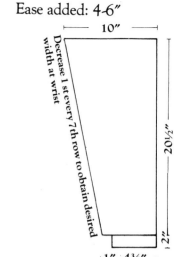

Men's sweater, medium size
Chest: 38-40″
Ease added: 4-6″

Decrease 1 st every 7th row to obtain desired width at wrist

25

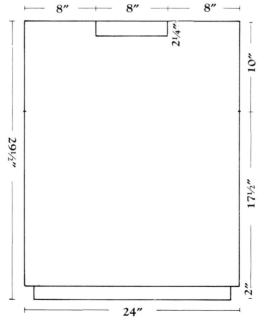

Men's sweater, large size
Chest: 41-43″
Ease added: 5-7″

Decrease 1 st every 7th row to obtain desired width at wrist

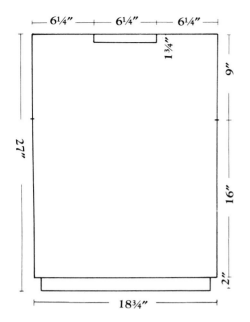

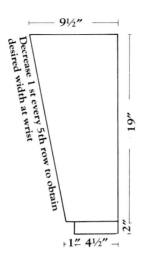

Teenagers' sweater
Chest: 32-34"
Ease added: 3½-5½"

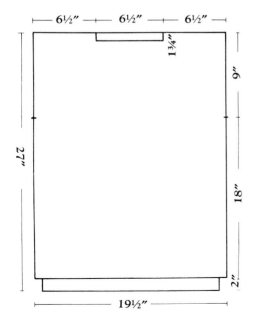

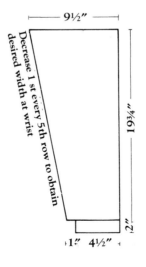

Women's sweater, medium size
Chest: 34-36"
Ease added: 3-5"

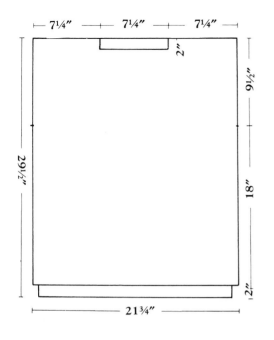

7¼"   7¼"   7¼"

2"

9½"

29½"

18"

2"

21¾"

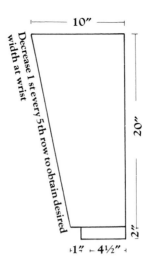

10"

Decrease 1 st every 5th row to obtain desired width at wrist

20"

2"

1"   4½"

Women's sweater, large size
Chest: 38-40"
Ease added: 3½-5½"

27

5½"   5½"   5½"

1¾"

6½"

19½"

11"

2"

16½"

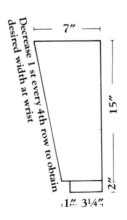

7"

Decrease 1 st every 4th row to obtain desired width at wrist

15"

2"

1"   3¼"

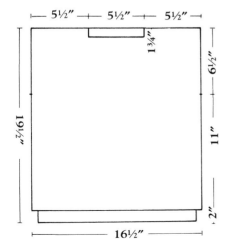

Children's sweater
Chest: 28-30"
Ease added: 3-5"

1 Termunten
2 Delfzijl
3 Usquert
4 Zoutkamp
  (Lauwersoog)
5 Moddergat/
  Paesens
6 Harlingen
7 Terschelling
8 Texel
9 Den Helder
10 Wieringen
11 De Rijp
12 Egmond aan Zee
13 Enkhuizen
14 Urk
15 Volendam
16 Marken
17 IJmuiden
18 Velsen
19 Amsterdam
20 Elburg
21 Harderwijk
22 Bunschoten
   Spakenburg
23 Noordwijk
24 Katwijk
25 Scheveningen
26 Maassluis

27 Vlaardingen
28 Delfshaven
29 Pernis
30 Zwartewaal
31 Brielle
32 Ouddorp
33 Goedereede
34 Stellendam
35 Middelharnis
36 Zierikzee
37 Bruinisse
38 Tholen
39 Bergen op Zoom
40 Colijnsplaat
41 Kortgene
42 Arnemuiden
43 Yerseke
44 Vlissingen
45 Breskens
46 Terneuzen

Fishing villages of the Netherlands.

Locations of fishing fleets, past and
present. The fishermen's sweaters for
which patterns are included in this book
are from the villages marked with
solid dots. ●

The Fishing Villages
and Their Sweaters

Four Fishermen in Bowlers

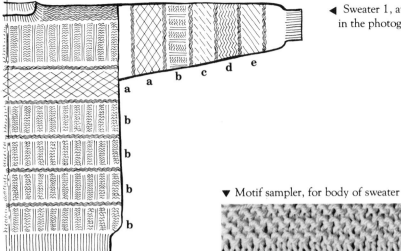

◀ Sweater 1, at left in the photograph

The names and home towns of these men are unknown. The picture was sent to me because the sweaters are so beautiful. During my research for this book I asked many people about these men— who they were and where they came from. It was suggested that they might have come from the islands of Zuid-Holland, because bowlers used to be worn there. (It was also suggested that they were from Noord-Holland, for the same reason.) Nobody was certain. During this time the group also acquired a name: first they were called simply "men with bowlers," then "the Dalton Gang." If any

▼ These four men are a mystery; no one knows where they came from or who they are.

▼ Motif sampler, for body of sweater

◀ Motifs for sweater 1

▶ Motif sampler, sleeve, sweater 1

▼ Motifs for the sleeve, sweater 1

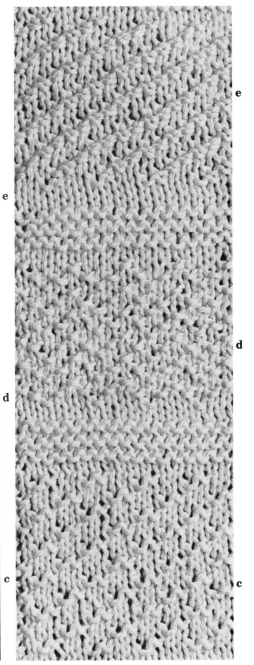

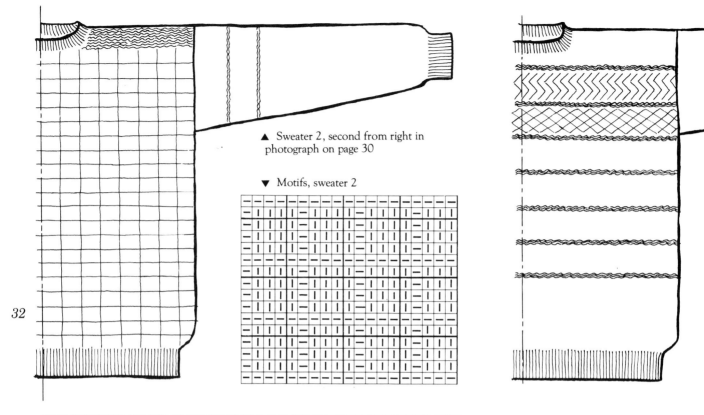

32

▲ Sweater 2, second from right in photograph on page 30

▼ Motifs, sweater 2

reader knows who these men are, or where they came from, please write to me!

It was impossible to work out a pattern for the second sweater from the left due to the poor quality of the photograph. A complete pattern is given for the sweater on the left in the photograph. The others are incomplete. The missing motifs can be filled in, using your own good judgment, with some of the other motifs shown. The motifs used here are all variations of knit and purl stitches.

◀ Sampler of motifs for sweater 2

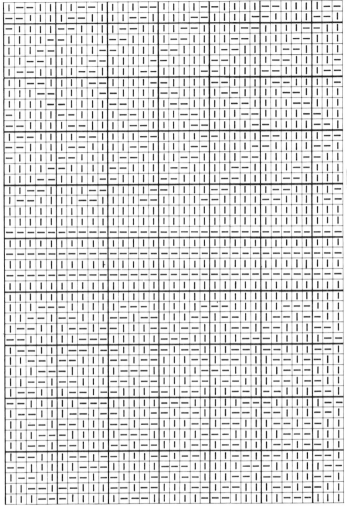

▲ Motifs, sweater 3

◀ Motif sampler, sweater 3

◀ Sweater 3, at right in the photograph on page 30

33

Rescuers and the Rescued

This picture was taken in 1907 to commemorate the successful rescue of the schooner *Doris*. On December 15th of that year the *Doris* had difficulties on the Westerschelde, one of the Dutch waterways. The rescue squad answered the call for help and saved the crew members. What happened afterward is unknown, nor is it certain that the whole crew was rescued. The most conspicuous figure in this picture is the little boy with the pinched face. He cannot have been over seven or eight years old when he survived this disaster with the other fishermen.

At that time it was not unusual for small boys to go to sea; tradition and strict necessity made this a common practice. The families were large, and usually lived in very small houses. The average house had one main room in which the family washed, cooked, and lived. The only other room was often an attic in which the children slept. The girls slept together, as did the boys.

When the father was away at sea, responsibility for the family rested solely with the mother. She not only had to take care of the house and the family, but she also had to earn money. The wages of the father were based on the earnings

▼ Many of these fishermen are wearing the so-called English sweaters. This sweater was originally knitted in England especially for Dutch fishermen. The whole sweater was in stockinette except for the God's Eye which adorns the front. In this picture are fishermen from different towns, including Arnemuiden (in the sweater with the blocks motif), and Katwijk (in the sweater with cables).

from the catch; a fixed income was nonexistent in the fishing industry. The mother's earnings were much needed.

Girls followed early in their mothers' footsteps. They took care of the infants and toddlers in the family, and shared in daily household tasks. During their "free" hours they were taught knitting and mending.

Boys filled their time differently, no household chores or knitting for them! They would go to sea and become fishermen. Their fathers and the other fishermen were shining examples.

There were, of course, schools which all children were obliged to attend. The importance of book learning was not always recognized. Playing hooky was a sport at which most fishermen's sons were masters. The logical solution was for a father to take his son to sea. The boy was taught a trade and was educated in the environment in which he would remain for the rest of his life.

This practice continues even today. But the age at which a boy might accompany his father on a fishing voyage was raised from seven to twelve, and it became mandatory that boys first finish elementary school. After the war, fishing industry schools were started, where the boys received a good education for five years. There were no problem teenagers in the fishing villages. Before they reached that age, they already had several sea voyages behind them.

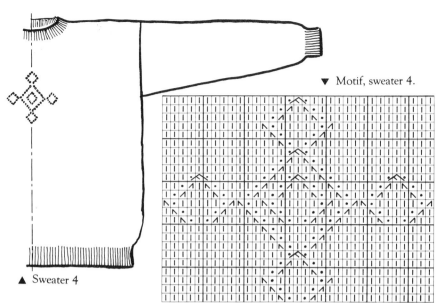

▲ Sweater 4

▼ Motif, sweater 4.

35

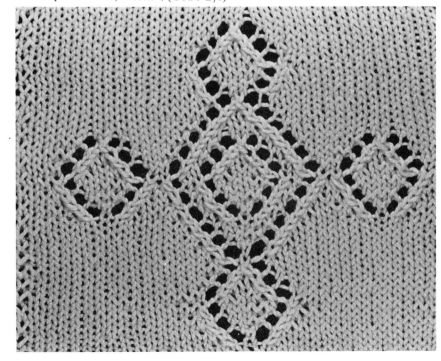

▼ Sampler of motif, sweater 4 (God's Eye)

Arnemuiden

At the beginning of this century in Arnemuiden only unpatterned dark blue sweaters were worn for work. Often the sweater was worn as a kind of vest under the jacket, and was not seen. It would have made little sense to go to the

▼ A group of fishermen at work in the harbor. The man on the right wears a sweater which strongly resembles felt: felting was a technique frequently used to make the knitwear windproof and water repellent.

trouble of knitting in motifs. The women of Arnemuiden at that time had little time and patience for knitting. In addition to being a housewife and mother, a woman often was a "fishwife" besides. That meant a long walk each day from Arnemuiden to Middelburg, carrying a heavy basket of fish to sell.

On the outbound trip, the fishwife often carried a weight of 176 pounds. After this heavy day's work the household chores would still await her, and preparation was necessary for the next day's trip to the city. Only on Sundays and holidays was there time to knit.

Knitting was regarded as a good way to rest without being idle. Women and young girls could be seen in those days in the doorways of their homes or strolling along the street while knitting stockings at the same time. Of all the knitting that had to be done, sweaters were only a small part. Stockings took up most of the knitting time; they wore out much faster and needed replacement more often.

Some years later, when the standard of living had improved somewhat, women had more time to devote to their handiwork. In the market places they began to see

fishermen from other places dressed in beautiful sweaters and so began to use motifs in their own knitting.

It is interesting that the knitters frequently used diamond motifs in their knitting. It is said that they copied those diamond motifs from the diamond patterns in the brick walls of buildings. That brickwork was done at a time when it was not yet possible to make large quantities of brick in the same color. There was variation in the temperature of the wood-burning ovens, and in the color of the loads of clay. The

▼ A fisherman from Arnemuiden with his wife. His sweater has no knitted motif at all, so was probably one of the early examples from Arnemuiden.

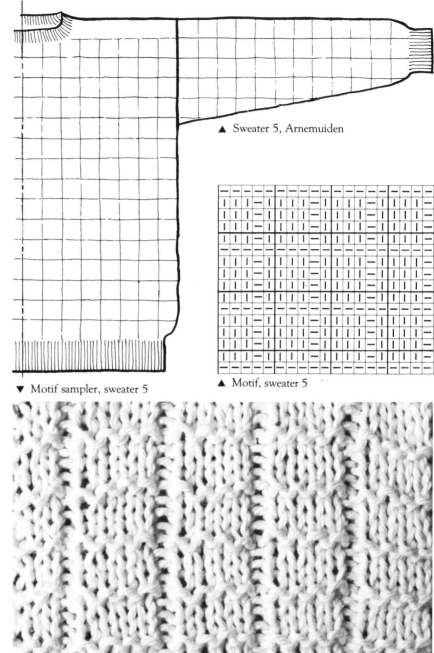

▲ Sweater 5, Arnemuiden

37

▲ Motif, sweater 5

▼ Motif sampler, sweater 5

bricklayers took advantage of the color variations, laying the bricks to form patterns of different colored diamonds.

Fishermen by then had begun to wear sweaters as outer garments, not hidden under jackets, and no longer were they worn just for heavy labor. They were worn over undershirts. The undershirt was made of red, gray or blue flannel, and had a small standing collar at the neck. The collar closed with beautiful buttons, so was allowed to show above the neck of the sweater. The neck of the sweater could be tightened with a drawstring. The drawstring had tassels on each end which hung down the front of the sweater. In the sweater color there was no variation: dark blue was worn up through the tight post-war years.

38

Men today seldom wear the original costume. The women are somewhat more faithful in this respect. Still, the original sweaters have not been forgotten. Stores feature dolls dressed in costume, including the sweater. This proves that in Arnemuiden the sweaters have been an integral part of the costume of men. Recently a new tradition has been established: a bridal couple receives as a wedding present a pair of dolls dressed in the original costumes.

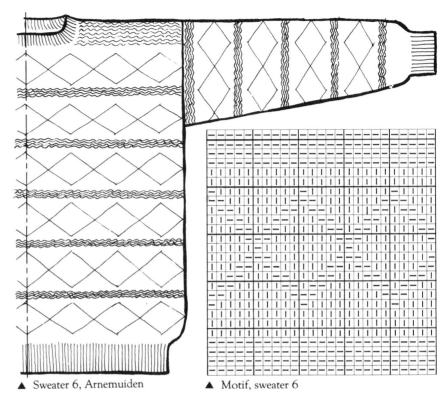

▲ Sweater 6, Arnemuiden   ▲ Motif, sweater 6

▼ Motif sampler, sweater 6

Bunschoten Spakenburg

Early in this century, sweaters already were popular among fishermen from these two villages near the IJsselmeer. (The IJsselmeer, a large body of water which was originally part of the Zuider Zee, was formed when a dike was built to dam the Zuider and reclaim its marsh for fertile farmland. A number of fishing villages became lake ports rather than seaports; consequently they lost their source of income.)

Their sweaters were cornflower blue, as were those worn on Urk. The fishermen owned two kinds of sweaters: a heavy one to wear at sea, and a thinner one for onshore wear: the Sunday sweater. The sea sweaters were "felted," treated in a special way to make them wind-and-waterproof. An oversized sweater was knit with heavy sajet, a sweater at least twice the desired size. The sweater was then submerged in a

▲ The current archivist at Bunschoten willingly contributed his school picture.

tub of hot water, and rubbed and punched until it shrank to half its original size. The result was a piece of clothing heavy as lead, water-

39

▼ Class picture from 1949. Many young girls were still wearing the traditional costume, even though the *kaper* (or tabard, a kind of vest) had nearly disappeared by then. The boys all wore hand-knitted sweaters.

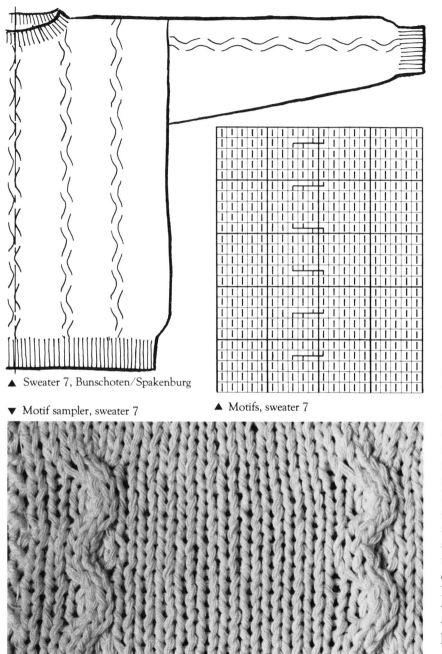

40

▲ Sweater 7, Bunschoten/Spakenburg

▼ Motif sampler, sweater 7

▲ Motifs, sweater 7

and windproof. For the Sunday sweater a thinner sajet was used, and this one was not felted. Fishermen kept their sea sweaters until they were completely worn out. Sunday sweaters were worn to church, and afterward to do small chores around the house. A Sunday sweater was never worn at sea, nor a sea sweater on shore.

A person in mourning dyed his cornflower blue sweater a darker marine blue. The dyed sweater was worn after the mourning period was over because it was nearly impossible to wash out the dye. After a period of time so many mourning sweaters appeared that the dark color had nearly become the fashion. Then marine blue sweaters became popular even with people who were not in mourning, and the original cornflower blue color nearly disappeared.

The sweaters were knitted in the round with five needles. A row of eyelet was knitted into the neckband, and through it was threaded first a shoelace, then later a piece of elastic, so that the neckband closed tightly. This was especially important for the felted sea sweaters. The neckband of these sweaters had to be wide enough that the head could pass through it easily. The felting process causes knitwear to lose its elasticity, and the wide neckband stayed open. So the shoelace was no unnecessary luxury.

The motif on the sweaters in these villages consisted of cables alternating with stockinette stitch.

Despite the many cable variations that evolved over the years, the overall pattern on sweaters from this area changed little, and it was always identified with these villages. Many stories are told about the fall of 1939 when a fisherman drowned in the IJsselmeer. By the end of that winter his body still had not been found. In May 1940 the war had begun, and the populations of both villages were evacuated to Enkhuizen, to the north. During the fourteen days they were there a body had washed ashore nearby, on the beach close to Medemblik. The body was identified as having come from Spakenburg or Bunschoten. This was determined by the color and motif of his sweater. After so long in the water the body itself was unidentifiable, but the sweater was still in good condition. The woman who had knitted the sweater recognized her work and knew for certain who the dead man was. They buried him in Medemblik.

After the war the style of the sweaters changed. It became fashionable to wear clothes similar to those worn by the British navy. Fishermen from Bunschoten and Spakenburg did not want to give up their traditional sweaters, but they also wanted to be fashionable. So they found a compromise: they cut slits in their own sweaters and installed zippers. That way the sweaters resembled those of the English navy somewhat, and their own traditional pattern lived on.

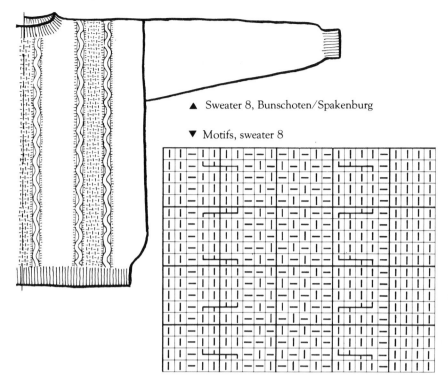

▲ Sweater 8, Bunschoten/Spakenburg

▼ Motifs, sweater 8

41

▼ Motif sampler, sweater 8

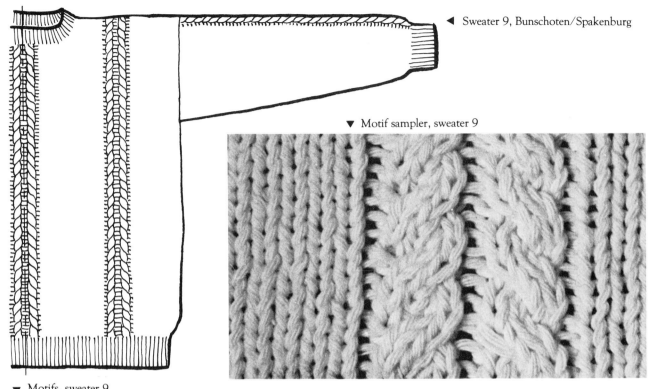

◄ Sweater 9, Bunschoten/Spakenburg

▼ Motif sampler, sweater 9

42

▼ Motifs, sweater 9

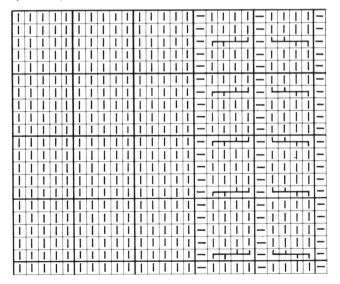

▼ Variation

Egmond aan Zee

In Egmond little girls were taught to knit when they were very young. As soon as their small fingers were limber enough they began by knitting socks. To inspire enthusiasm for the work, their mothers would conceal pennies in the ball of sajet. Since sajet was sold in skeins which had to be wound into balls before knitting, it was not difficult to hide a few pennies in the ball. The little girl was allowed to buy candy with her pennies as soon as she had finished knitting the ball of yarn. To get their rewards as quickly as possible the girls would stand and knit on their front stoops before going to school in the morning.

Sweaters were uncommon in Egmond because, for many, the large quantity of sajet needed for a sweater was just too expensive. Consequently there is no real sweater tradition in Egmond.

This motif consists of a variation of knit and purl stitches.

▶ Lifeguard at Egmond. In addition to keeping an eye on the bathers, he also rented wicker beach chairs and kept the beach clean.

▲ Sweater 10, Egmond aan Zee
▼ Motif sampler, sweater 10

▲ Motifs, sweater 10

Goedereede-Havenhoofd/ Ouddorp/ Stellendam

The people of Goedereede were fishermen and farmers. The fishermen lived near the pier and kept to themselves. They fished along the coast, mainly for shrimp. The fishermen wanted to go farther away, to the English coast. To do this they needed larger boats meeting the requirements for deep sea fishing. They couldn't afford to build new boats, so had to find another solution. Finally a fleet of the right boats was located in the village of Moddergat. There, in the northernmost corner of the country, a terrible disaster had occurred, and nearly the entire male population of the village had perished. There were no longer enough men to sail the local fleet; so the boats had to be sold. "One man's loss is another's gain" is a phrase that certainly holds true in this case; the tragic death of the Moddergat fishermen made it possible for the fishermen of Goedereede-Havenhoofd to develop their deep sea fishing industry.

As was often the custom among fishing families, the young boys went to sea with their fathers at an early age. As soon as they finished elementary school they began their

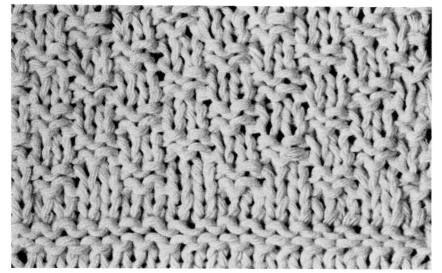

adult lives. Later the founding of fishing industry schools changed that custom, and after elementary school boys were required to attend school for an additional five years before they were allowed to go fishing. As far back as anyone can remember, the fishermen from Goedereede-Havenhoofd wore sweaters with their own distinctive motif. They also wore billowing pants with a flap in front. Over the sweater was worn a jacket of brown duffel which they called a "monkey jacket." No one could remember where the name came from, or how it originated. On their heads they wore caps with brass buttons on each side. When a man went into mourning he painted his cap buttons black. Shiny things and mourning are not compatible. The earnings of a fisherman were meager, and the family income was supplemented in a number of different ways. One source of extra money was the business of peeling shrimp and collecting the shells. The shells were sold to factories for processing. Shrimp peeling was done during the time from November to March when bad weather made fishing expeditions impossible.

▶ Four fishermen from the islands of Zuidholland had themselves photographed in Rotterdam after a good catch in 1911. The men standing were from Goedereede-Havenhoofd; the seated man on the left is from Ouddorp, and the one on the right from Stellendam.

▲ The crew of the *Solo* of Rotterdam. Most of them came from the islands of Zuidholland.

In addition to their paid part-time work, fishermen often walked the beaches to find anything useful which might have washed ashore. Here, as in other coastal villages, beachcombing was a serious occupation. Even driftwood was valuable. It was used to repair houses or as firewood. Once the villagers found on the beach a number of barrels—still full of wine. Everyone, including the children, drank it, and the women boiled it down to make jelly. The story is still told today of the children lying drunk on the beach along with the adults.

Young girls here attended sewing and knitting school where they were taught the tricks of the textile trade. Beginning at age five or six they used every spare moment to make clothing or household articles like stockings, undershirts, blankets and sweaters.

The motif and the pattern of the sweaters typical of these villages was still familiar to the women here, although such sweaters have not been worn in recent years. First a ribbing was knit of 2 knit stitches and 2 purl, then a section in plain stockinette. The unpatterned sections were knit to save on the sajet; a plain piece of knitting requires less yarn than one with a motif. Then came a decorative horizontal band bordered by garter stitch; then the main motif, which con-

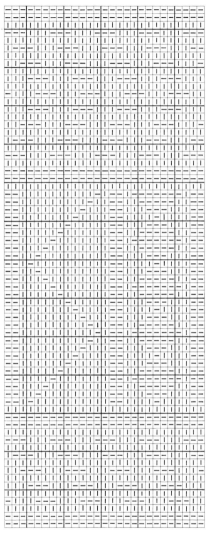

▲ Motifs, sweater 11

sisted of vertical strips of zigzag and diamond patterns. The neckband had a row of eyelet for a drawstring with a pompon on each end. The

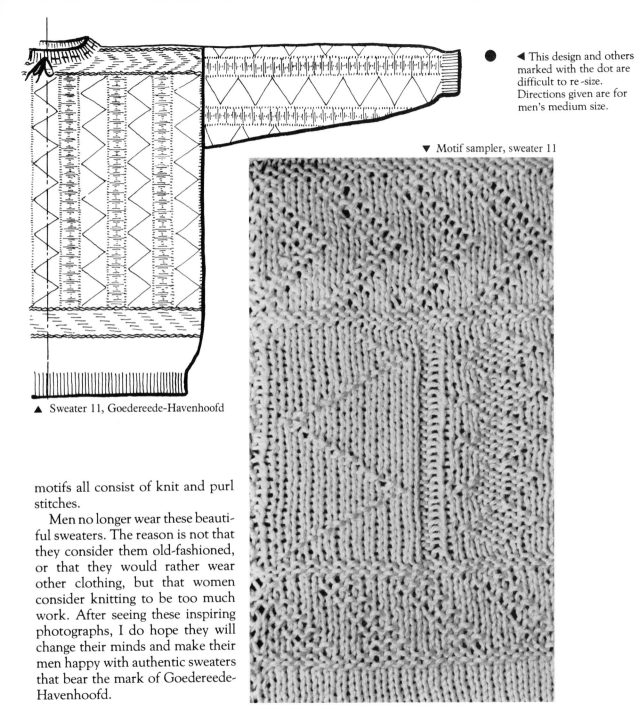

◀ This design and others marked with the dot are difficult to re-size. Directions given are for men's medium size.

▼ Motif sampler, sweater 11

▲ Sweater 11, Goedereede-Havenhoofd

motifs all consist of knit and purl stitches.

Men no longer wear these beautiful sweaters. The reason is not that they consider them old-fashioned, or that they would rather wear other clothing, but that women consider knitting to be too much work. After seeing these inspiring photographs, I do hope they will change their minds and make their men happy with authentic sweaters that bear the mark of Goedereede-Havenhoofd.

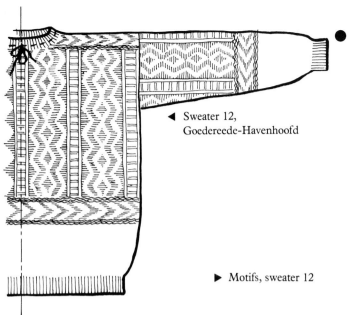

◀ Sweater 12,
Goedereede-Havenhoofd

▶ Motifs, sweater 12

48

◀ Motif sampler, sweater 12

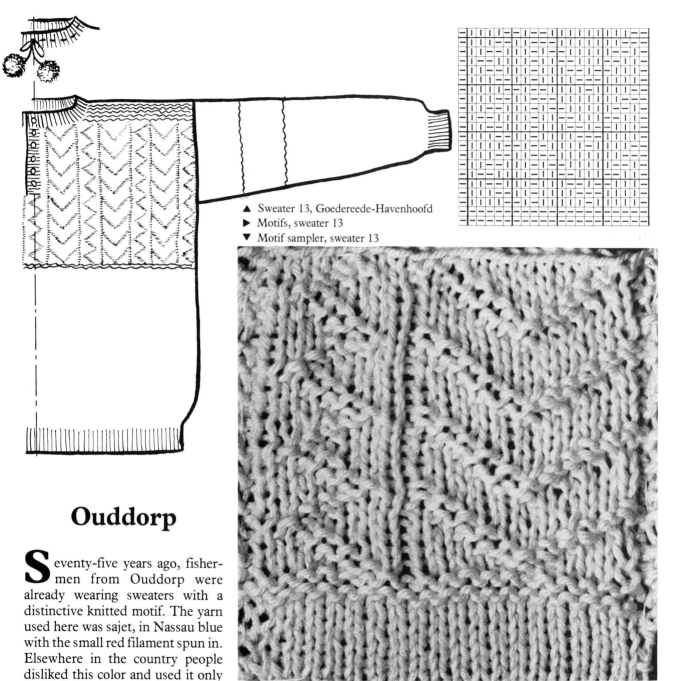

▲ Sweater 13, Goedereede-Havenhoofd
▶ Motifs, sweater 13
▼ Motif sampler, sweater 13

Ouddorp

Seventy-five years ago, fisher-men from Ouddorp were already wearing sweaters with a distinctive knitted motif. The yarn used here was sajet, in Nassau blue with the small red filament spun in. Elsewhere in the country people disliked this color and used it only

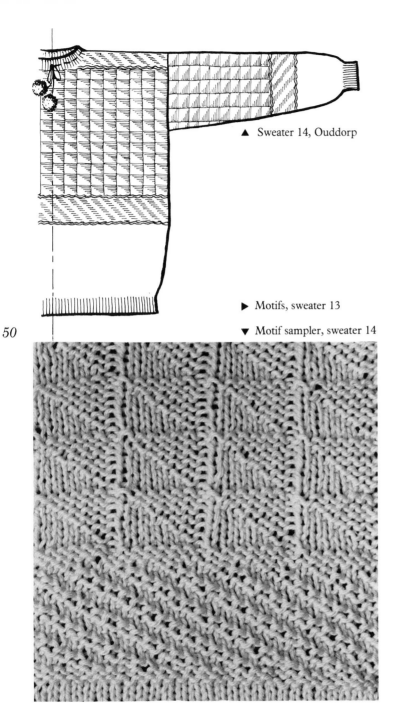

▲ Sweater 14, Ouddorp

▶ Motifs, sweater 13

▼ Motif sampler, sweater 14

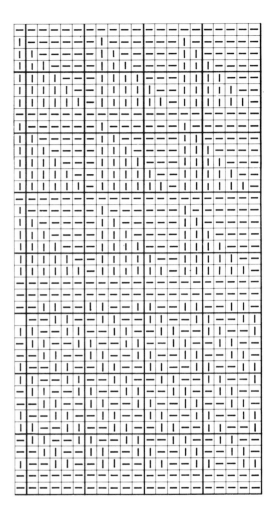

for knitting stockings. Here in Ouddorp knitters appreciated this very special color and preferred it for knitting sweaters.

Little girls learned to knit and sew at an early age. They began, at the age of six, to attend sewing and knitting school for two hours every day after their regular classes ended.

A spinster from the village earned her living by conducting this school. At the beginning of the school year the girls brought three yards of yellow cotton fabric and enough yarn to knit all the pieces they would make that year. With the cotton, a sewing sampler piece was made on which the girls practiced seams, hems and buttonholes. Then at the end of the year an undershirt was made with the remaining cloth. Some of the yarn was used to knit a swatch. Holes were cut into it, and the girls were taught to darn them neatly. The little girls also learned how to knit socks with different kinds of heels and toes. The older girls knitted samplers with different stitches and motifs.

Eventually all this knowledge and expertise was applied to many pieces of handiwork. Nearly all clothing and household linens were made by the women themselves. There were work gloves from blue sajet for the men, undervests of beige sajet for the winter and of white cotton for summer, white cotton blankets, and of course a great many socks and stockings of all kinds and in all sizes. Sweaters were knitted in Ouddorp as long ago as in 1872. One woman was still able to tell me exactly how a sweater had to be made: first a ribbing of K2, P2; then about 4 inches of stockinette, then a band of garter stitch, and after that a small border. This border consisted of 2 knit and 2 purl stitches. These were moved over one stitch in each row

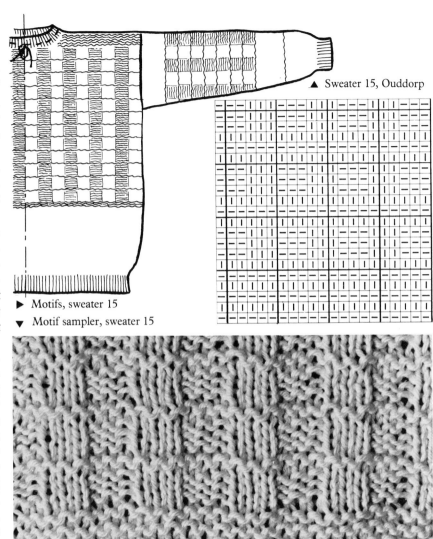

▲ Sweater 15, Ouddorp

▶ Motifs, sweater 15

▼ Motif sampler, sweater 15

so a slanting line resulted. Then the pattern of squares began, each square consisting of 7 stitches. The sleeves were of a similar design: a stockinette section, a border and then a pattern. There was also a garter stitch border across the shoulder. All motifs were made up of knit and purl stitches.

No photo of this sweater could be found at the time, so the sweater shown here was reconstructed from

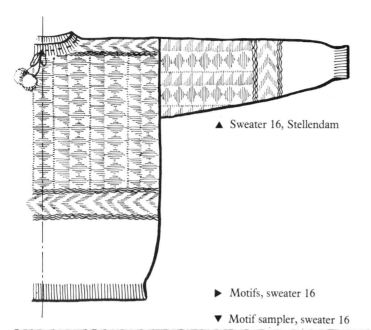

▲ Sweater 16, Stellendam

52

▶ Motifs, sweater 16

▼ Motif sampler, sweater 16

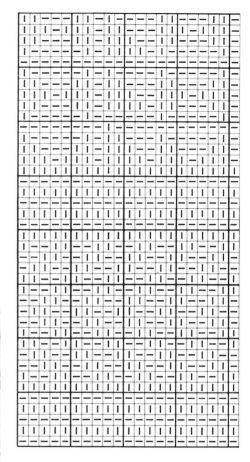

the village woman's very clear instructions. Later, another woman did find a picture of four fishermen, one of whom was wearing a sweater in the pattern described to me.

The neck of the sweater was finished with a ribbing in which a row of eyelet was knitted. A twisted string went through the eyelet and had a pompon on each end. Not every man cared for pompons, so the drawstring sometimes ended in tassels instead.

IJmuiden

People's opinions about IJmuiden are divided, I discovered during a visit to the local senior citizens' complexes. The women were adamant: "IJmuiden does not exist, therefore there are no real IJmuideners." When I showed surprise they explained that IJmuiden, like the adjacent communities of Velsen and Noordwijk, did not come into existence until the digging of the canal which connects Amsterdam with the North Sea. People who now live in IJmuiden originally were from Egmond, Katwijk or Velsen, and came to IJmuiden as dredgers when the canal was dug. Many Scots and Belgians immigrated at the same time. Therefore it seems impossible to have a "traditional" sweater from IJmuiden. Yet at the local archives photographs were found of men wearing sweaters with a character all their own. So the fishermen of IJmuiden must have had their own sweater pattern, despite what the local women said. The motifs used in IJmuiden were a knit/purl design with cables on either side.

53

▲ Young fishermen show off an especially good catch.

▶ The fish auction at IJmuiden.

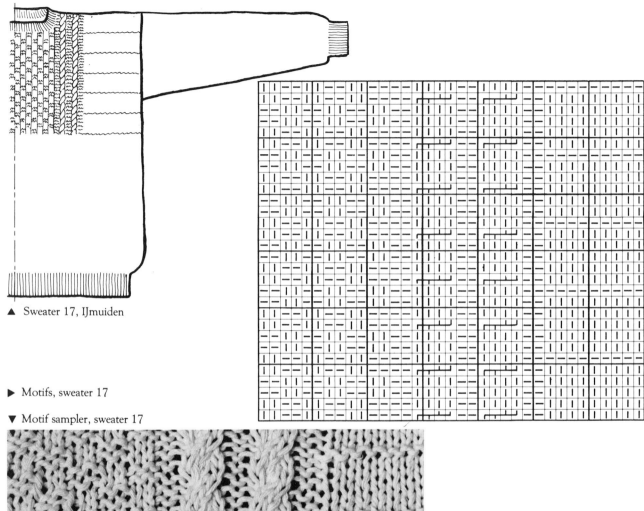

▲ Sweater 17, IJmuiden

▶ Motifs, sweater 17

▼ Motif sampler, sweater 17

Katwijk

Not until after the First World War were sweaters worn in Katwijk. Before that time the men wore a baize undershirt, and over it a *hemdrok*, a roomy sleeveless overshirt of black fabric trimmed with red braid. After the war ended the *hemdrok* was gradually replaced by the sweater. At first sweaters were worn exclusively as work clothing but later became acceptable for everyday wear.

The motif of the sweater shows that it is a fairly recent design. The first sweaters were modelled after the English workmen's smocks. The more common the sweater became, the more it took on a character of its own, and the less its motifs resembled those of the original smocks. The sweater of Katwijk shows no evidence of having evolved from the smock.

The motif covers the entire sweater, front and back, and above and below the armhole. The material used here was again sajet. The

▶ Family of four. The older boy seems very grown up with the cigar in his hand. This certainly was not a faked pose; he probably had already made several sea voyages and had acquired the experiences of a grown man.

▲ These two fishermen were brothers, originally from Zeeland. During a period of unemployment they left their home to find work elsewhere. After many years their mother received this picture and knew that her sons were alive and well. Although the picture was taken in IJmuiden, the sweaters show that the men sailed with the Katwijk fleet.

▲ These two young fishermen are busy sealing the barrels of cured herring. To protect their clothing from the brine, they wear aprons of oilcloth.

◀ Boys from Katwijk in the harbor of Lerwick in the Shetland Islands. They were away from home many months at a time, sometimes for the whole summer. The mother, who stayed behind, sent a small boy to sea and welcomed home a man.

▲ This fisherman's clothing came from different places. His sweater is the pattern of Katwijk, while his hat and trousers originated in Urk. This happened often when fishermen had to find work away from their home ports. After a period of time they adopted the styles worn in their new ports; in this man's case, the sweater.

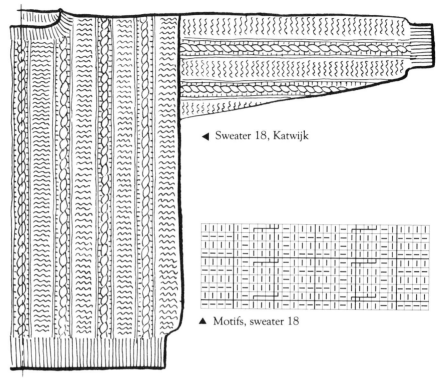

◄ Sweater 18, Katwijk

▲ Motifs, sweater 18

▼ Motif sampler, sweater 18

sweaters were knitted from black or Nassau beige sajet, while the beautiful Nassau blue was used only for stockings.

The motif consists of cables with bands of garter stitch between them, or bands of garter stitch with stockinette between them.

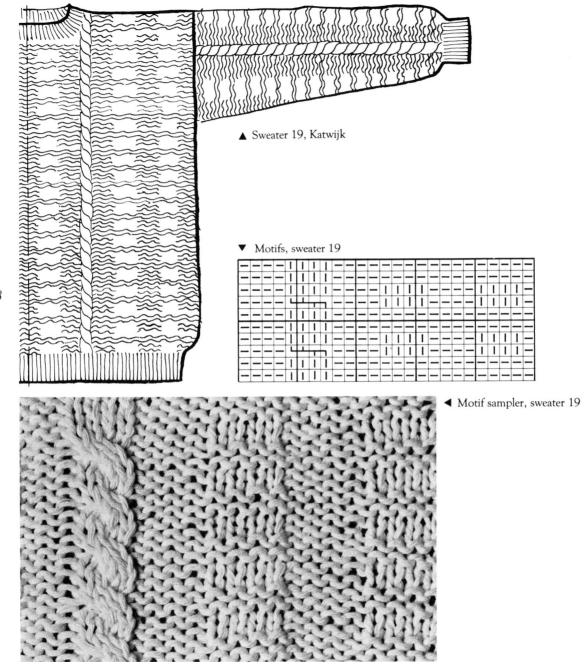

58

▲ Sweater 19, Katwijk

▼ Motifs, sweater 19

◄ Motif sampler, sweater 19

Maassluis

The clothing of these men shows that sweaters were not always part of a specific costume. Here the sweater was worn with *burgerbroek*, trousers worn by the middle class. Even so, the sweater had a distinctly local motif and was considered a costume especially for fishermen. Horizontal fishbones, sometimes interrupted, are featured on the sweaters of Maassluis.

▲ An old fisherman and his wife.
▼ The herring catch was put into barrels as soon as possible.

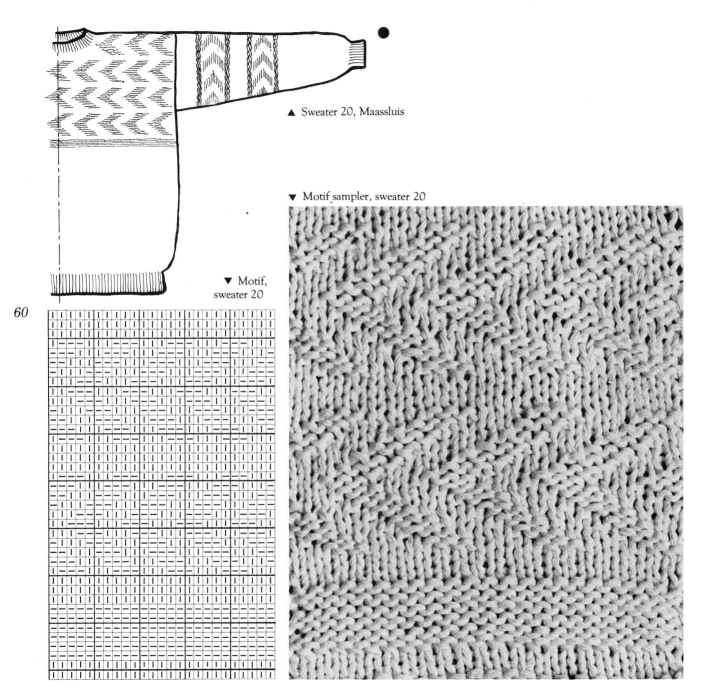

▲ Sweater 20, Maassluis

▼ Motif sampler, sweater 20

▼ Motif,
sweater 20

60

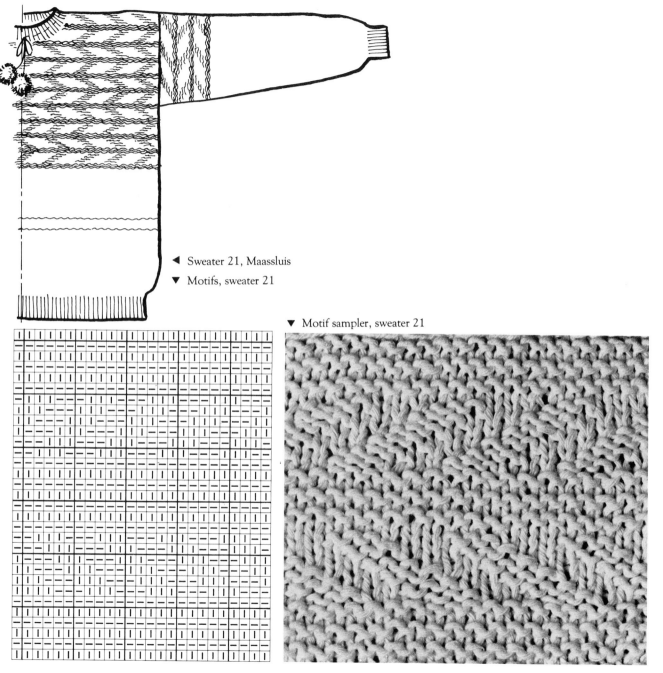

◀ Sweater 21, Maassluis

▼ Motifs, sweater 21

▼ Motif sampler, sweater 21

Middelharnis

The sweaters from Middelharnis were black or dark blue and knitted from 4- or 5-ply "Mercurius" sajet. The front and the sleeves were knitted in a ribbed pattern. This motif was knitted in Patent stitch of K3, P1. In the front was a placket which buttoned. The buttons on everyday sweaters were of strong bone or mother-of-pearl. The Sunday sweater sometimes had silver buttons from Zeeland. The Patent stitch can't be shown with a graph. Instructions for knitting the Patent stitch are on page 24.

62

▶ Two young fishermen after their first voyage on the *Middelharnis II*; named after the village.

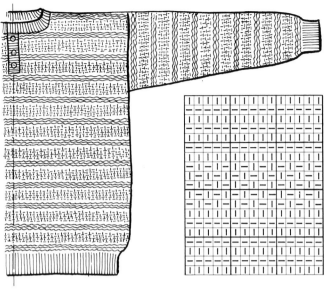

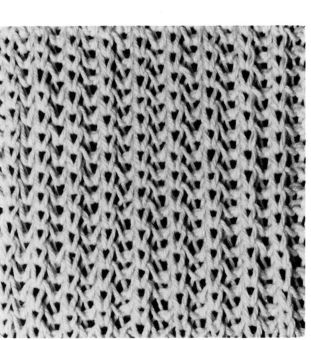

▲ Sweater 22, Middelharnis   ▲ Motifs, sweater 22

▶ Motif sampler, sweater 22

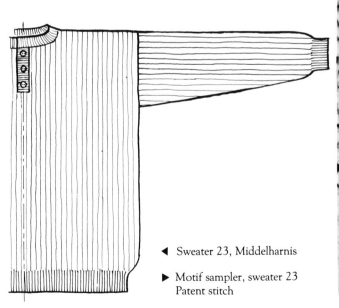

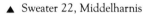

◀ Sweater 23, Middelharnis

▶ Motif sampler, sweater 23
Patent stitch

Moddergat/ Paesens

In Moddergat knitting was not exclusively a craft for women. The men also were very skilled knitters; they even developed a technique to knit on frames. This technique was used mainly for mats, which had small pompons knitted on them. They also knitted caps to which they attached small pompons, made in the same way as were those for the mats.

Here, too, sweaters were made of dark blue sajet and had drawstring necklines with small pompons at the ends of the drawstrings. This sweater had a smooth center front panel with a knit and purl pattern on either side.

64

▲ A fisherman and his wife at home.

▶ Two fishermen. The one on the left wears a knitted sweater and cap; the one at right poses in his undershirt.

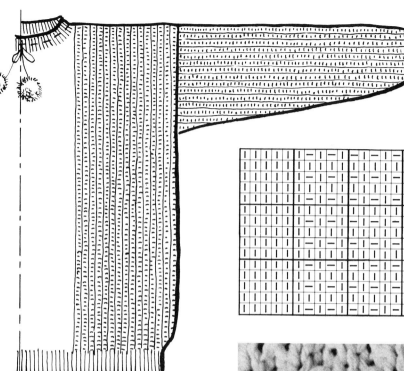

▲ Sweater 24, Moddergat/Paesens

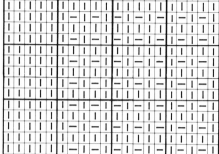

◀ Motifs, sweater 24

▼ Motif sampler, sweater 24

66

◀ Motifs, sweater 25

▲ Sweater 25, Moddergat/Paesens

▶ Motif sampler, sweater 25

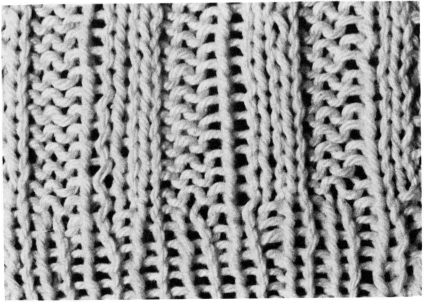

Noordwijk

The traditional sweater motif of Noordwijk is completely different from all other motifs used in the Netherlands. It is a bobble made by increasing and decreasing stitches. It is possible that this motif originates not in Great Britain, but in Denmark.

▶ A number of women in this picture are wearing dresses with square yokes, called *jas met Bata*.

▼ Crew of the lugger *Noordwijk I*, which sailed the North Sea around 1910.

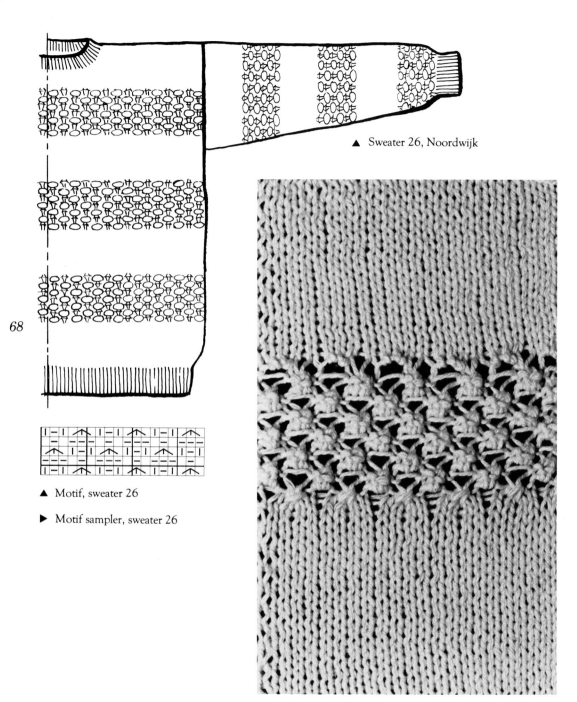

68

▲ Sweater 26, Noordwijk

▲ Motif, sweater 26

▶ Motif sampler, sweater 26

Pernis

Pernis, on the island of IJssel-monde, has been inhabited since 1300. Originally it belonged to the manor Putten, the realm of the earls of Putten. The original population occupied itself only with farming, but a natural disaster changed this. A severe gale changed the coastline and created a new harbor. The people from Pernis used it gratefully, and some of them took up fishing. Eventually, boats were built and more and more men from Pernis went to sea. After 1700 the fishing industry of Pernis played an important role in supplying fresh fish to the rest of the country.

It is certain that the fishermen of Pernis have been wearing sweaters from the time their fishing industry began. For them there was no changeover from jacket or smock to the sweater.

The fishermen from Pernis had been in contact with British fishermen since early times, so may have adopted their costume sooner than did other Dutch fishermen. The sweater from Pernis still shows

▶ This young man, with his hat at a cheerful tilt, was obviously doing well. In addition to his magnificent sweater, he wore a new pair of trousers, a beautifully made watch chain, and shoes of felt. These shoes, which resembled slippers, were very fashionable at that time as onshore wear.

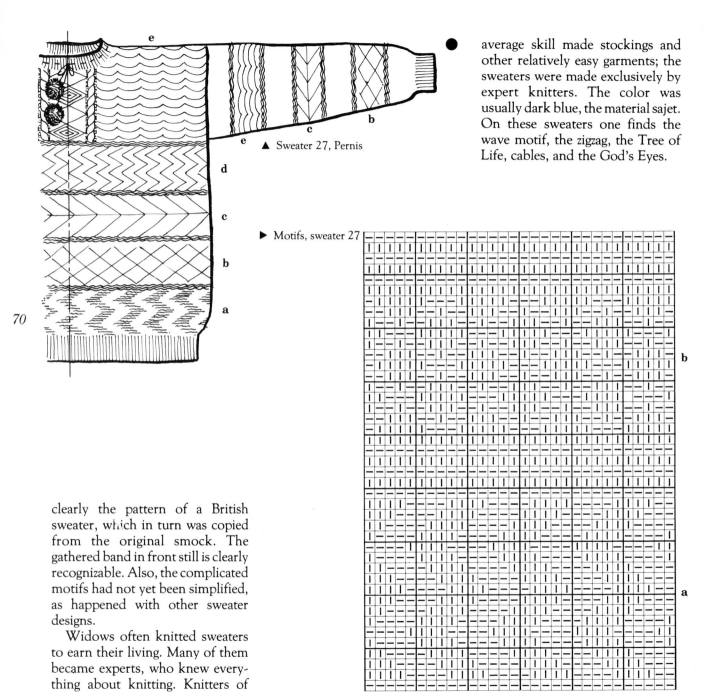

▲ Sweater 27, Pernis

▶ Motifs, sweater 27

average skill made stockings and other relatively easy garments; the sweaters were made exclusively by expert knitters. The color was usually dark blue, the material sajet. On these sweaters one finds the wave motif, the zigzag, the Tree of Life, cables, and the God's Eyes.

clearly the pattern of a British sweater, which in turn was copied from the original smock. The gathered band in front still is clearly recognizable. Also, the complicated motifs had not yet been simplified, as happened with other sweater designs.

Widows often knitted sweaters to earn their living. Many of them became experts, who knew everything about knitting. Knitters of

▶ Motif sampler, sweater 27

▼ Continuation of motifs for sweater 27

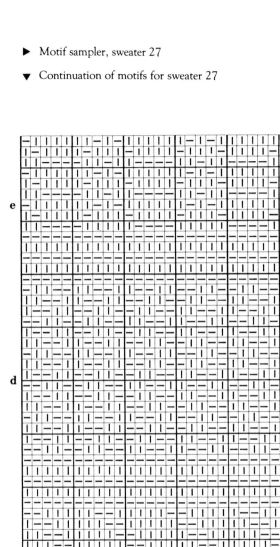

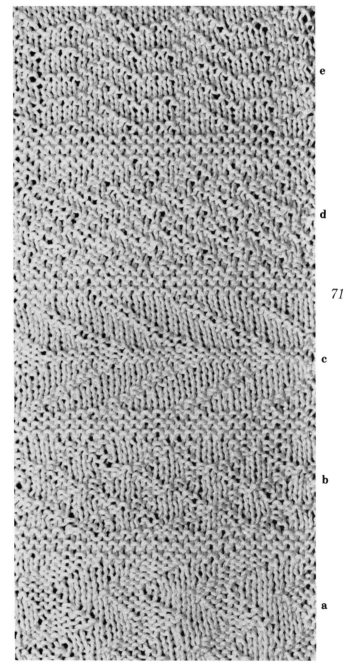

e

d

71

c

b

a

◀ Center motif,
sweater 27, Pernis

◀ Sampler of center
motif, sweater 27

Scheveningen

Scheveningen is one of the ports where the traditional sweaters are still worn. There are a few noticeable differences between those worn before and after the Second World War. Before the war black or dark blue sajet was used, afterward knitters began to make sweaters of the same wool which was used for socks, sometimes in a gray color. Before the war the neck ribbing was folded inward and sewn in place; after the war neck ribbing was knitted longer, folded outward, and no longer sewn in place.

The motifs and their placement remained unchanged. The body of the sweater was knitted in plain stockinette nearly halfway up, then the motifs were begun. All sweaters had to have cables, although the spacing between them might differ once in a while. Under the cable pattern was a zigzag band which marked the beginning of the pattern. Those zigzag bands were not always knitted the same way, but from a distance there is no apparent difference. A fisherman from Scheveningen is always recognized immediately by his sweater because all the sweaters from his village look alike.

As soon as a girl gave her "yes" to a fisherman and the wedding date was set, she would begin a sweater for him. This special sweater had to

▶ These retired fishermen, wearing their authentic sweaters, were photographed especially for this book. The sweater patterns are found on pages 74-76.

▼ A group of Scheveningen fishermen in the harbor of Lerwick, in the Shetland Islands. As early as 1500, Dutch fishermen sailed to the Shetlands. The area was "discovered" during the time when the Dutch and British were fighting over fishing rights off the English coast. The Dutchmen searched for new fishing grounds farther north, and eventually reached the Shetland Islands. They have maintained good relations with the inhabitants of the islands all through the centuries.

74

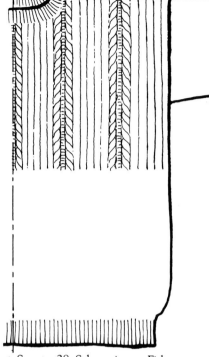

▲ Sweater 28, Scheveningen. Fisherman at left in photo on page 73.

▲ A beautiful photograph from a glass plate: two fishermen from Scheveningen and two from Urk, each in his own local costume. It is possible that they sailed on the same boat and there became friends. It was very common for fishermen to sail on boats from other ports. If a fisherman were unemployed he would look elsewhere for work rather than wait for work to become available in his home port. Sometimes, too, a particular port became unprofitable, was closed, and its fleet moved to another harbor. Patterns for these four sweaters are found on pages 77 through 80.

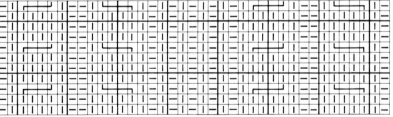

▲ Motifs, sweater 28
▼ Motifs, sweater 29

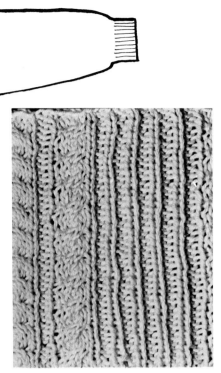

▲ Motif sampler, sweater 28

be completed prior to the wedding day so she could give it to him as a present. She knitted into the sweater long hairs which she pulled from her head. This not only strengthened the yarn, but resulted in a very personal and romantic garment through which she bound herself closely to her man.

The men of Scheveningen continue to wear their sweaters faithfully, even though the ones made now often are knitted of synthetic yarn.

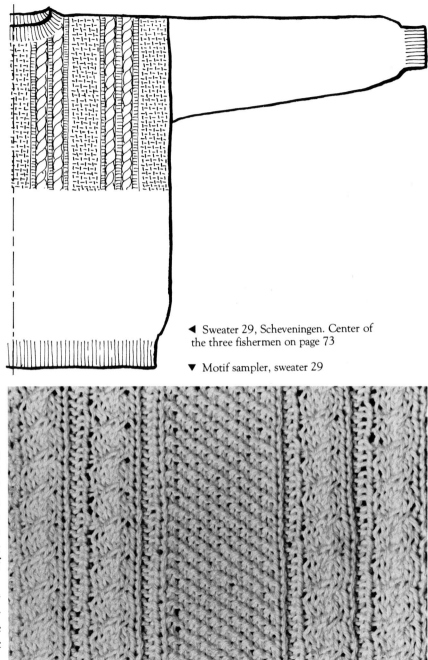

◀ Sweater 29, Scheveningen. Center of the three fishermen on page 73

▼ Motif sampler, sweater 29

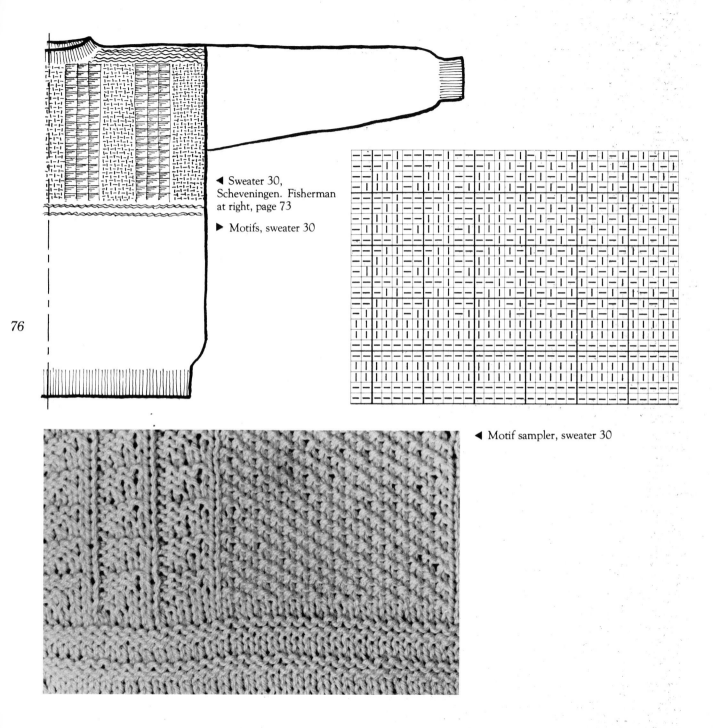

◀ Sweater 30,
Scheveningen. Fisherman
at right, page 73

▶ Motifs, sweater 30

◀ Motif sampler, sweater 30

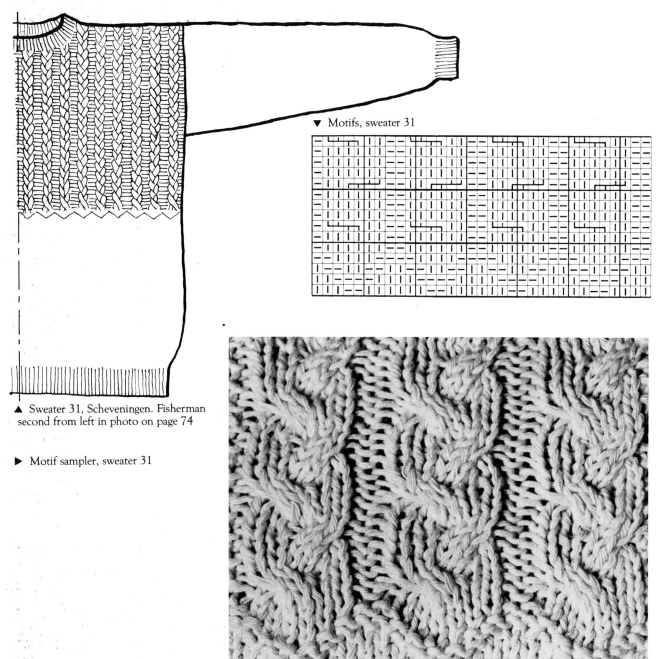

▼ Motifs, sweater 31

▲ Sweater 31, Scheveningen. Fisherman second from left in photo on page 74

▶ Motif sampler, sweater 31

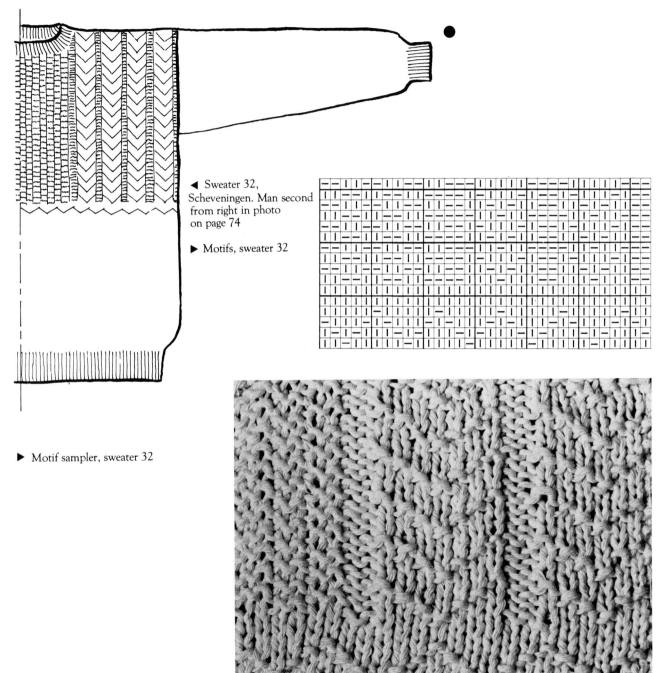

◀ Sweater 32,
Scheveningen. Man second
from right in photo
on page 74

▶ Motifs, sweater 32

▶ Motif sampler, sweater 32

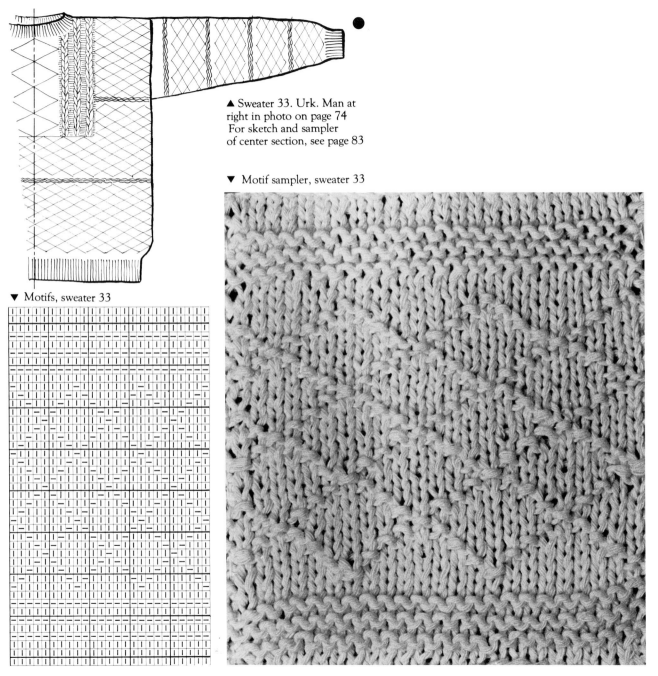

▲ Sweater 33. Urk. Man at
right in photo on page 74
For sketch and sampler
of center section, see page 83

▼ Motif sampler, sweater 33

79

▼ Motifs, sweater 33

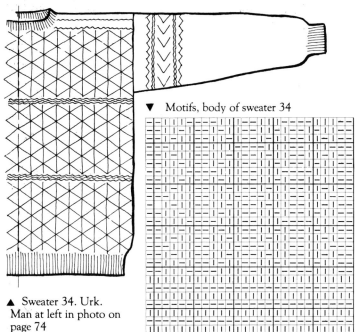

▲ Sweater 34. Urk.
Man at left in photo on
page 74

▼ Motifs, body of sweater 34

▲ Sleeve motifs, sweater 34

▼ Motif sampler, body, sweater 34

▼ Motif sampler, sleeve, sweater 34

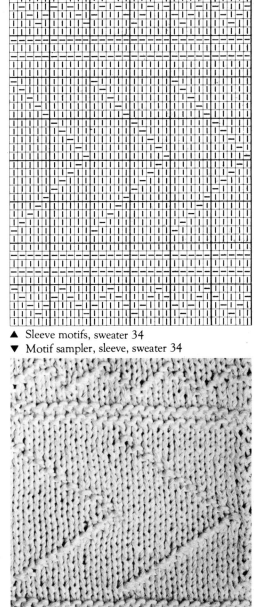

Urk

The women of Urk all agree that their fishermen have always worn sweaters. This was the case even back when Urk was still an island in the Zuider Zee. Sweaters were worn by men who fished locally, and also by those who went to fish for whales.

Men from Urk could be easily recognized because the same combination of motifs was always used in the sweaters. In the center front were flowers, or God's Eyes; on the sides were small points, or flags,

▼ A fisherman from Urk in the full glory of his costume. In addition to the beautiful sweater he wears silver buttons on his trousers and neckband. Around his neck is a traditional kerchief of black satin.

with a double cable. Even though none of the patterns or motifs were ever written down, nearly every woman can describe exactly how to knit such a sweater.

In addition to sweaters in Urk's own pattern, the so-called English sweaters were worn here too. They are well known throughout the Netherlands and are knitted in plain stockinette with only a God's Eye motif on the front. These sweaters

were either purchased or handmade.

In Urk, sweaters were always constructed in the same manner. A tube was knitted with four needles, then stitches were picked up at the armholes to knit the sleeves. Needle and thread were never used in the making of a fisherman's sweater.

The prevailing sweater color is cornflower blue, a color typical of that side of the IJsselmeer. Black was the color for mourning; the mourning sweaters were made of black wool. Occasionally a work sweater might be knitted in the color usually reserved for underwear, a sort of beige. One woman who did this told me she had three fishermen in her household and so to tell the sweaters apart she gave her husband a blue sweater, one son a black one and the other son a beige one.

Sweaters were worn not just for work, but also on Sundays and holidays. The "good" sweaters differed from the work sweaters: they were made with fine two-ply wool yarn, while the work sweaters were of heavy four- or six-ply wool.

The men of Urk also wore beautiful stockings with knitted lace motifs. These stockings were, like their sweaters, an integral part of the traditional costume. In earlier times it was the custom to wear lace stockings over a pair of plain black ones. The Sunday stockings had an open motif, and those for work a closed one. In previous centuries it was common to wear one pair of

82

▲ Two fishermen from Urk having a conversation. By our standards these sweaters were worn a little too tight. This photograph dates back to the time that a sweater was really considered an undergarment.

stockings over another. Floors of houses at that time were not carpeted, but were tiled. In addition, doors did not close tightly and there were always drafts. To combat the cold, people wore two, three, or even four pair of stockings, one over the other.

Women of the village remember that the yarn used for sweaters was

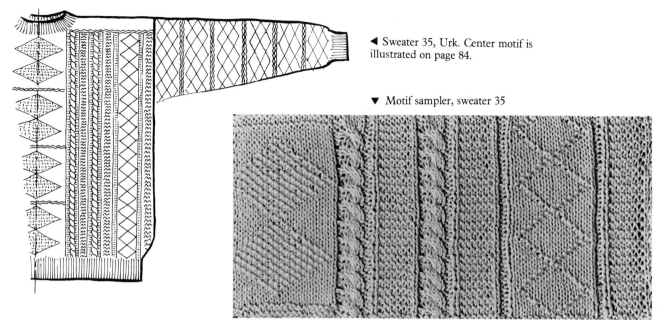

◀ Sweater 35, Urk. Center motif is illustrated on page 84.

▼ Motif sampler, sweater 35

83

▼ Motifs, sweater 35

sajet, an inexpensive wool available from peddlers in any color they needed. Before the days of peddlers, yarn was probably spun at home. The sajet is remembered with sadness. It was a wool that felt warm but was also quite strong. These days, synthetic yarns are used much of the time.

A man from Urk was quickly recognized by his sweater, not only in his own town, but outside the village as well. There was another very special value attached to the sweater: that of the union of a wife with her sailing husband. A woman who spent many hours knitting a sweater for her husband put into it

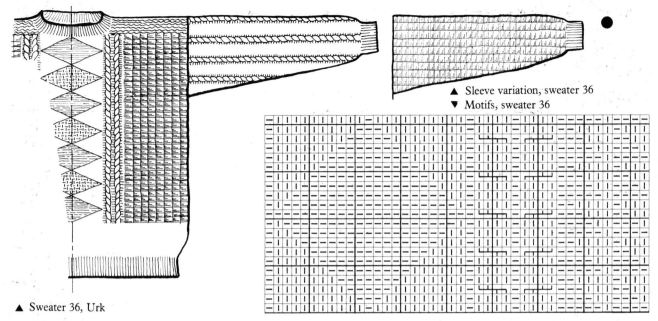

▲ Sleeve variation, sweater 36

▼ Motifs, sweater 36

▲ Sweater 36, Urk

▼ Motif sampler, sweater 36

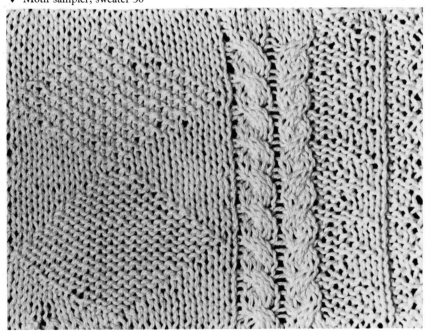

not only her expertise, but also her love for him. Even though the same patterns and motifs were used on all the sweaters, a woman made sure to give her husband something that was different from what the other fishermen had. She might embroider his monogram on the front, or use special stitches or stitch combinations. This way she would be able to recognize her husband under any circumstances. And on board ship it would be impossible to have a misunderstanding about the ownership of a sweater. No strange man would put on her sweater by accident.

There are many stories concerning the individual qualities knitted into the sweaters. A recent tale, from the sixties, involves a fishing boat which disappeared at sea. Neither it nor the crew could be found. After hearing the news, one of the fishermen's wives began to leave her door open day and night, so that if her husband should come home he would not find the door closed. One day the boat was found, with the bodies of the men aboard. Before the bodies were buried at sea the sweaters were removed and taken back to Urk to be returned to the fishermen's wives. The woman who had left her door open recognized her own knitting, and knew then that her husband would not return. The sweater was buried, the piece of clothing that had been worn closest to her husband's heart.

God's Eyes, cables and flags are the motifs which characterize the sweaters of Urk.

Velsen

Originally Velsen was a community in which half the population was farmers, and the other half involved in the fishing industry. During the digging of the canal from Amsterdam to the North Sea, the town of IJmuiden came into being, and Velsen was incorporated into it. Nevertheless, the natives of Velsen deny any connection with IJmuiden.

The sweaters of Velsen are plain: bands in a variation of knit and purl stitches alternating with bands of garter stitch.

▶ A picture from the time when photographers used glass plates. Because a long exposure was necessary the model had to hold onto something, lest he move and spoil the picture.

▲ This kind-looking man was a cod cutter in Velsen. His sweater is the same as that worn by the man shown on the previous page, whose place of origin could not be determined. Because of the sweater pattern, we assume that he also came from Velsen. The motif of the sweater is very much like that worn in Staithes, England.

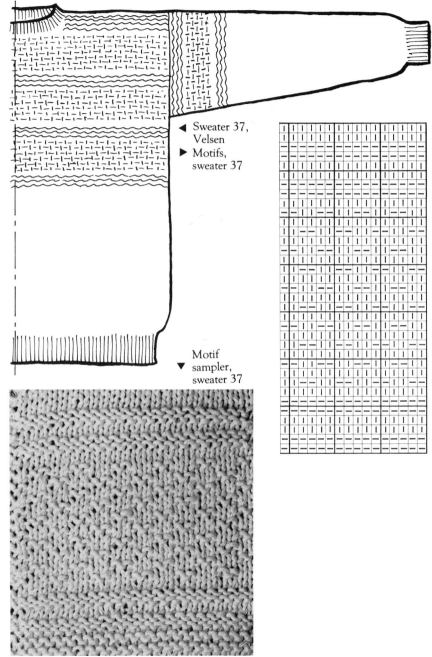

◀ Sweater 37, Velsen

▶ Motifs, sweater 37

▼ Motif sampler, sweater 37

Vlaardingen

Fishermen of Vlaardingen wore sweaters knitted from Nassau blue sajet. The remarkable quality of this wool was its red hue, caused by the small red filaments spun together with the yarn. In some places knitters disliked the color, and it was generally considered a color worn by the lower classes.

The neckband of the sweater was folded inward and sewn in place. In early days a drawstring was then put through it; later this was replaced with a piece of elastic.

Despite the fact that there were a number of professional knitters in Vlaardingen, the housewives also knitted sweaters. The sweater pattern common to Vlaardingen was complicated and required a great deal of knitting expertise. A professional knitter could knit a large man's sweater in one week, quite an accomplishment when one considers the complexity of the motifs.

Thin sajet was supplied by the customer, or bought for him by the knitter. The knitter spent long hours working in front of her window to finish the piece on time. Using 2 to 2.5mm needles (or about U.S. size 0), she knitted the sweater all in one piece. One must realize that by the time she began the last sleeve, about two pounds of wool hung on the needles!

▶ This woman, who posed with her children in the early 1900s for an inexpert photographer, was the last professional knitter in Vlaardingen. An old citizen of Vlaardingen remembered when he and his co-workers used to pass by her window at five o'clock in the morning on their way to the early shift. Often she would still be up, working at her knitting. The men would knock against the window and call: "Are you *still* knitting?"

▲ The photographer's client was allowed to choose the background he liked best. The backgrounds were painted on cloth panels, which hung from the ceiling on rolls. He also was allowed to choose between a chair and a console for support. This fisherman from Vlaardingen chose a draped curtain as his backdrop.

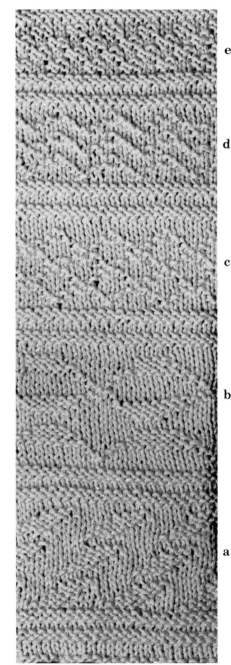

e

d

c

b

a

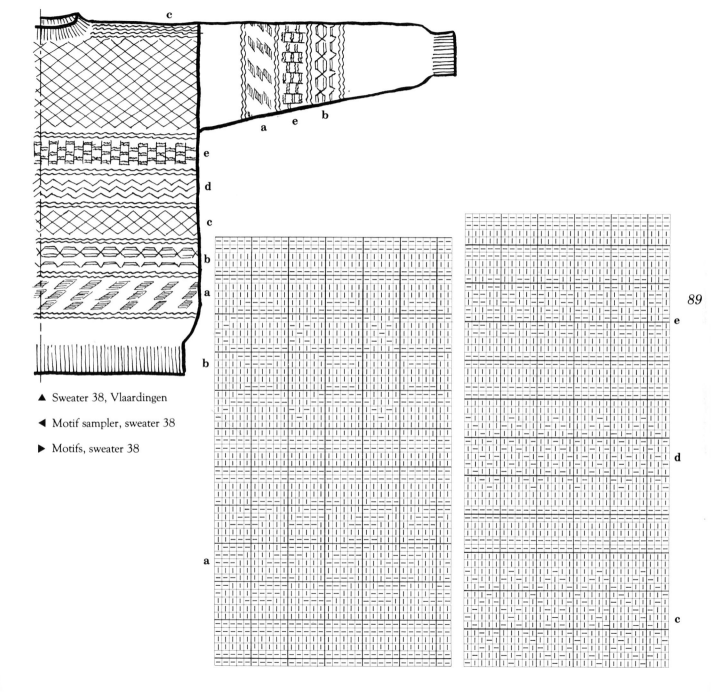

▲ Sweater 38, Vlaardingen

◄ Motif sampler, sweater 38

▶ Motifs, sweater 38

89

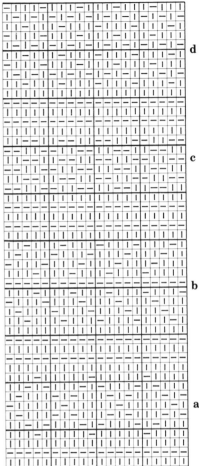

▲ Motifs, sweater 39

◀ Perhaps this picture was taken to immortalize the knitting of an especially fine sweater.

▶ Complete crew of the lugger *Vlaardingen 192*, which sailed on the North Sea around 1905. Recognizable by their sweater motifs are two men from Vlaardingen and one from Noordwijk.

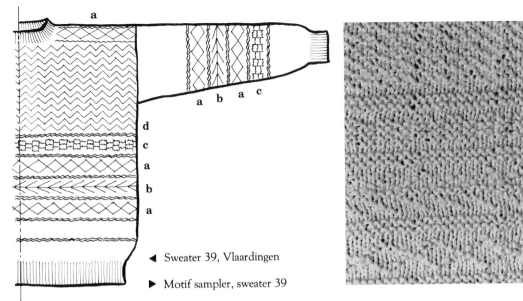

◀ Sweater 39, Vlaardingen

▶ Motif sampler, sweater 39

Volendam

Fishermen of Volendam began to wear sweaters in fairly recent times. The first sweaters, smoothly knitted blue work sweaters, appeared in the village around 1910. For about ten years these nondescript sweaters were worn on board ship for heavy work, and nobody paid them much attention. A fisherman was recognized at sea by the rest of his clothing; not by his sweater. Then around 1920 fishermen began to wear black sweaters with a motif of horizontal stripes. Men wore the new style hesitantly at first, and it is not clear what brought about this change in fashion.

In the beginning, these black sweaters were worn alternately with the blue work sweaters. They were "handyman's" clothes, not to be worn for heavy work, yet not part of the Sunday finery. The term handyman's clothing was common in the Netherlands before World War II. It referred to clothing worn during the week, but not on holidays. At that time the work day was divided into two parts. From early in the day until midmorning, both men and women did the "dirty" work, or heavy chores. For that kind of work one wore old clothes. After those jobs were finished one washed up and put on handyman's clothes. In these clothes one did the lighter tasks, ran errands, and received company. An unwritten rule of etiquette prohibited appearing on the street in work clothes. And to visit someone or receive a guest while wearing work clothes was considered highly improper.

Knitting was done both by women and men, but there was a difference. Men only knitted nets, while the women knitted clothes. No Volendam man would have looked askance if asked whether he

▼ Three fishermen from Volendam in their traditional costume. They still wear the typical sweaters today, and are among the last to do so.

could knit. He knew the questioner referred to the knitting of nets.

When the wearing of sweaters became common practice, children also started to wear them. From birth until their third year they wore dresses. Then the boys received their first real men's pants, and a black sweater. Girls began to wear dresses with long sleeves. A man's clothing would change little during the rest of his life.

The traditional sweater of Volendam was knitted, like all fishermen's sweaters in the Netherlands, of sajet. It was made with four or more needles, in the round. Here again, no written pattern was used. The rule prohibiting seams in fishermen's sweaters was followed here as it was elsewhere in the country. Here, too, eyelets were knitted in the neckband so the band could be tightened with a shoelace. The ends of the shoelace were tied in back and the knot hidden in the neckband.

Over the sweater was worn a loose collar with golden buttons. Leaving the sweater neckband in plain view was considered untidy; it had to be covered neatly.

An authentic fisherman's sweater from Volendam, one knitted by hand in the traditional pattern, was called a "sweater;" one knitted by machine or in accordance with a fashion pattern was called a "frock." The sweater was worn exclusively as part of the costume, and the frock was part of the "civilian" wear.

Horizontal strips of stockinette, alternating with knit/purl variations, are characteristic of the sweaters from Volendam.

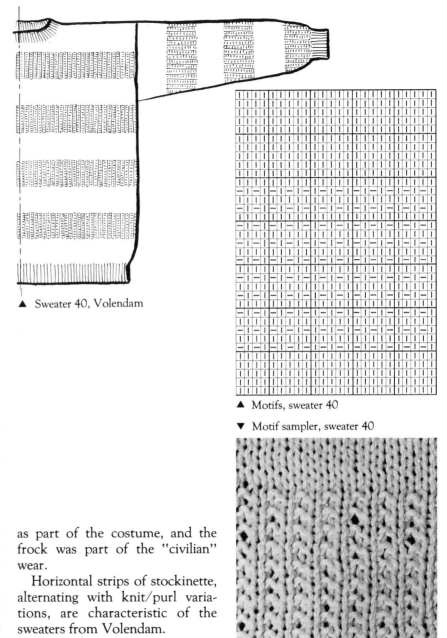

▲ Sweater 40, Volendam

▲ Motifs, sweater 40

▼ Motif sampler, sweater 40

93

Zwartewaal

This photograph had belonged to a deceased woman resident of Zwartewaal, Mrs. Geritje Smit. She was the last descendant of a fisherman's family. This is really the entire story of the picture, because only one fisherman, the man on the right in the back row, could be recognized. He was Mrs. Smit's father, also a native of Zwartewaal. The other men are unknown, and the occasion for the photograph could not be discovered. It is possible that the other fishermen in the picture came from other villages.

▼ A picture from Zwartewaal about which little can be said. The man in the back row is from Zwartewaal. It is not known where the other men came from.

Postscript

Many people were involved in the creation of this book. During the three years it took to gather all the information, many letters were written back and forth, telephone conversations took place, and people were visited. Nearly everyone involved in this research reacted very positively and did his best to gather the necessary material. For that I am most grateful, because by myself I would not have been able to bring this project to a good end. After the idea was born I took it to my friend Scarlett Houtman. She was enthusiastic from the beginning, and accompanied me to the first few fishing villages on my list. Her mother, Mrs. P. Houtman-Geurtzgen, supported me with patience and understanding. The first drafts were read and corrected by Ms. R. Berkvens.

The following people received me cordially and helped me tremendously in many ways. I hereby express my thankfulness, also, to anyone whom I may have omitted.

Henriette C. van der Klift-Tellegen

Mrs. Blauw	IJmuiden/Velsen City Archives
Mr. A. Boogerman	Middelharnis
Mr. J. Borsboom	Vlaardingen
Mrs. Geertvliet	Pernis
Mr. Groen	Moddergat-Fiskers huske (model house)
Mrs. Groenendijk	Goedereede-Havenhoofd
Mrs. de Haas	Noordwijk
Mrs. Harrebomee-Moonen	Open-air Museum, Arnhem
Mr. M. Harvey	Darlington, England
Mr. W. Helm	Documentation Center of the Delta Area of Zeeland, Middelburg
Mrs. Hengeveld	Harlingen, Museum Hannemahuis
Mr. P. Hop	Spakenburg
Mr. de Jager	The Hague
Mr. Koelewijn	Bunschoten City Archives
Mrs. H. Kramer	Urk
Mrs. Komtebedde-Lodder	Ouddorp
Mrs. Maljers	Arnemuiden
Mr. K. Mol	Voldendam Museum
Mrs. de Nooyer	Arnemuiden
Mr. D. Schaap	Abcoude
Mrs. J. Schilder	Volendam
Mrs. J. Schraal	Urk
Mr. Schuur	Elburg City Museum
Mrs. Steur	Volendam Museum
Mrs. Struijs	Vlaardingen
Mr. M. Struijs	Vlaardingen City Archives
Mrs. Taal	Scheveningen
Mr. Kees Tanis	Goedereede-Havenhoofd
Mrs. van Urk	Urk
Mr. C. Varkevisser	Katwijk Association
Mrs. M.H. van Velzen-Zuydwijk	Scheveningen Museum
Mrs. J. Verboon	Vlaardingen Fishing Museum
Mr. Verdon	Breskens
Mrs. S. Vons	Amsterdam, Institute for Pre- and Protohistory
Mr. P. Voogt	Vierpolders
Mr. G. Wakker	Urk
Mr. Zwaan	Bunschoten
Mr. A. Williamson	Lower Hillhead, Lerwick, Shetland Islands
Mr. P. van der Zwan	Urk

Reading List

Verleden Land — H.F. Bloemers, L.P. Louwe, Kooymans — H. Sarfatij-Meulenhof Informatief

Everyday Costume in Britain — Audrey Barfoot — Batsford

Halen en Brengen — Dick Schaap — A.W. Sijthoff

Traditional Knitting Patterns — James Norbury — Dover Press

Patterns for Guernseys, Jerseys and Arans — Thompson-Dover Press

A Sacred History of Knitting — H.E. Kiewe — Art Needlework Industries Ltd., Oxford

Urk zoals het reilt en zeilt — Visserijmuseum Urk

Vikingen — Frank Donvan, Thomas D. Kendrick — W. Gaarde, The Hague

Aran and Fair Isle Knitting — Golden Hands

A Day in the Life of a Victorian Farmworker —Frank Huggett — George Allen & Unwin

Smocks — Maggie Hall — Shire Albums

Groot Museum Book — J. Elffers, M. Schuyt, A. Overbeek — Landshoff

Visserskind — Visserijmuseum Vlaardingen

Jerseys Old and New — La Societe Jersiaise

Al zwerf ik op de baren — Jan Houter-Wereldvenster

Een sociale zaak —Visserijmuseum Vlaardingen

Scottish Home Industries — Alexander Ross — Scolar Press — Ilkley, Yorkshire

De zeevaarders — Het onstaan der mensheid — Time-Life Books, Amsterdam

Brood uit het water — Ferdinand van den Oever —Callenbach, Nijkerk

Historisch Jaarboek — Gemeentearchief Vlaardingen

Hollanders in Shetland — Adrian J. Beenhakker

The History of Handknitting — Michael Harvey —Patons Publications

Breien in Europa — Die Masche

Vissers van de Noordzee — Dr. J.P. van de Voort — Boekencentrum, The Hague

De Nederlanden, ruim honderd jaar geleden — N.V. Foresta

100 verbeeldingen van Ambachten — Johannes en Caspaares Luiken — te Amsterdam

Visserijgeschiedenis van Kampen — Stedelijk Museum Broederpoort

Photo Credits

City Archives of Vlaardingen: pages 2, 55, 69, 85, 87, 88, 90, 91

Documentation Center of the Delta Area of Zeeland, Middelburg: pages 8-9, 34, 36

City Archives of Velsen: pages 53, 86

G. Wakker, Urk: pages 13, 57

Fishing Museum of Vlaardingen: pages 30, 56, 67, 73, 81, 94

City Museum of The Hague: page 7

Victoria and Albert Museum, London: page 10

Mrs. C.F. Canter Cremers - van der Does, The Hague Collection, Hermitage Museum, Leningrad: page 11

De Nederlanden, ruim honderd jaar geleden, N.V. Foresta: page 14

Mrs. de Nooyer, Arnemuiden: page 37

City Archives of Bunschoten: page 39 (upper)

P. Hop, Spakenburg: page 39 (lower)

Mrs. Groenendijk, Goedereede-Havenhoofd: page 45

Kees Tanis, Goedereede-Havenhoofd: page 46

Mrs. Geervliet, Pernis: page 56 (top center)

National Towing Service Museum, Maassluis: page 59

Mr. Boogerman, Middelharnis: page 62

Fiskers Huske, Moddergat: page 64

Volendam Museum: page 92

P. van der Zwan, Urk: page 43